Decision Basis Evaluation

Decision Basis Evaluation
Toward Safe Machine Intelligence

Stephen P. Hershey

VERTILAB

Published by VERTILAB
Sarasota, Florida, USA
www.vertilab.com

First edition: October 2015

ISBN 978-0-9966971-0-1

Library of Congress Control Number: 2015913841

Typeset in LaTeX.
Copyeditor: Sue Hargis Spigel

In Memoriam
Grandmother Mary
February 24, 1913 - May 19, 2014

I have never entered into any Controversy in [defense] of my philosophical Opinions; I leave them to take their Chance in the World. If they are right, Truth and Experience will support them. If wrong, they ought to be refuted and rejected. Disputes are apt to sour one's Temper and disturb one's Quiet.

— Benjamin Franklin, *Letter to Lebègue de Presle* (1777)

Contents

List of Figures

List of Tables

1 Introduction

Although the prospects of directly specifying an [artificial intelligence's] decision theory are perhaps more hopeful than those of directly specifying its final values, we are still confronted with a substantial risk of error. Many of the complications that might break the currently most popular decision theories were discovered only recently, suggesting that there might exist further problems that have not yet come into sight. The result of giving the [artificial intelligence] a flawed decision theory might be disastrous, possibly amounting to an existential catastrophe.

— Nick Bostrom, *Superintelligence* (2014)

1.1 Overview

Decision basis evaluation is the process by which a decision maker (DM) evaluates the basis of its decision after experiencing the consequence of implementing its decision. Informally, if the DM is surprised by the consequence, it negatively evaluates its decision basis. If the DM is not surprised, it positively evaluates its decision basis. This book provides a formal analysis of this intuitive idea.[1]

When a DM negatively evaluates its decision basis, it can perform a *decision repair* operation in the hope that its subsequent decision basis evaluations will be positive. The purpose of decision basis evaluation is error detection, whereas the purpose of decision repair is error prevention.

This book introduces the Administer Treatment (ADTR) decision problem as a convenient means of studying decision basis evaluation. In this decision problem, a DM named Amy is a doctor who can *will* the administration of one among several alternative treatments to her patient. Amy must decide which treatment *to will*.

A DM can be classified as either *animal* or *machine.* An animal DM (whether human or nonhuman) is the product of natural evolutionary processes. A machine DM is designed and implemented by a human or another machine.

A DM can also be classified as either *autonomous* or *nonautonomous.* An autonomous DM operates free of human control or influence, while a nonautonomous DM incorporates a human into its decision process. For example, a DM that submits its decision to a human for approval before implementation is nonautonomous.

An *autonomous machine decision maker* (AMDM) that routinely performs decision basis evaluation and decision repair may be less hazardous to public safety than one that does not. As an initial step in the study of the relationship between decision basis evaluation and public safety, Amy has been implemented as an AMDM in a software testbed called the *Decision Basis Evaluation Testbed* (DBET).

In a typical DBET session, the DBET user (called Zoë in this book) first configures a set of parameters associated with Amy and her simulated environment. These parameters are collectively called the *case.* Zoë then *runs* (or *executes*) the case. During case execution, Amy performs one or more *decision cycles*, where each decision cycle includes acquiring a decision basis, making a decision, implementing the decision, evaluating her decision basis, and performing a decision repair operation when appropriate. The output produced by DBET during the execution of a case is called a *trace*. A complete description of Zoë's interaction with DBET, including the specification of case parameters and the production of traces, is called a *transcript.* This book employs 16 traces to support its analysis of decision basis evaluation.

1.2 Organization

This book is organized into 14 chapters and four appendices:

· Chapter 2 describes the approach to proposition evaluation employed in this book.

· Chapter 3 describes the decision cycle sequence, a framework for a DM's decision process.

· Chapter 4 describes the ADTR decision problem.

· Chapter 5 describes decision basis evaluation in detail for two ADTR cases.

· Chapter 6 conceptualizes decision basis evaluation information flow.

· Chapter 7 explores decision basis evaluation when Amy alone reports to Zoë.

· Chapter 8 describes Amy's decision making algorithm as implemented in DBET, and discusses the relationship between decision basis evaluation and rational decision making.

· Chapter 9 discusses the relationship between decision basis evaluation and truth. An *infallible* agent named Betty is introduced as a counterpart to the *fallible* DM Amy.

· Chapter 10 explores decision basis evaluation when both Amy and Betty report to Zoë.

· Chapter 11 discusses the relationship between a *DM's alternative set* and the *perfect alternative set*.

· Chapter 12 consolidates the ideas introduced in the preceding chapters.

· Chapter 13 takes an informal look at decision repair.

· Chapter 14 provides some concluding remarks.

· Appendix A discusses cases where the DM's will is unrealized.

· Appendix B provides an example of a complete description of a decision basis norm.

· Appendix C discusses utility function prediction.

· Appendix D provides a list of abbreviations used in the book.

Notes

[1]Decisions are sometimes evaluated based on the outcome. If the outcome is desirable, the decision is evaluated as *good*; if the outcome is undesirable, the decision is evaluated as *bad*. This decision evaluation strategy is not examined in this book.

Decisions are also sometimes evaluated as *rational* or *irrational*. This decision evaluation strategy is not examined in this book.

2 Proposition Evaluation

This chapter is an introduction to proposition evaluation. Section 2.1 provides three introductory proposition evaluation examples. Section 2.2 presents a proposition evaluation algorithm and provides five examples of its use.

2.1 Introductory examples

This section uses three examples to introduce the approach to proposition evaluation employed in this book. Each example features five agents:

Eva: evaluates the proposition

Priya: supplies Eva with the proposition

Nancy: supplies Eva with the norm

Fay: receives the result of Eva's proposition evaluation

Rita: sets the state of the part of the world that the proposition and norm are about

These agents appear only in this chapter, but each has a counterpart in the analysis of decision basis evaluation presented later in the book.

In the examples in this chapter, the proposition and norm each make a claim about the shape of a marble token that has been placed in a bag. The token shapes and associated abbreviations used in the examples are shown in Figure 2.1.

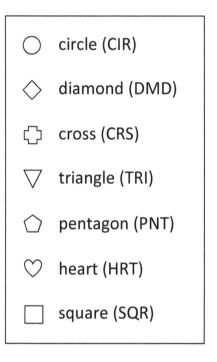

Figure 2.1: Token shapes

Each example will be expressed concisely using the following notation and terminology:

- β means *an accurate description of the shape of the token inside the bag.*

- The claim 'β ∈ {TRI}' means *an accurate description of the shape of the token inside the bag is an element of the set consisting of the single element TRI.* This is an expression of *certainty.* A more compact equivalent English translation is *the shape of the token inside the bag is TRI.*

- The claim 'β ∈ {CIR DMD CRS}' means *an accurate description of the shape of the token inside the bag is an element of the set consisting of the elements CIR, DMD, and CRS*. This is an expression of *uncertainty*. A more compact equivalent English translation is *the shape of the token inside the bag is CIR, DMD, or CRS*.

- In order for a claim to be a proposition, a norm for the claim must be identified by an agent. Similarly, in order for a claim to be a norm, a proposition must be identified for the claim by an agent. All propositions and norms are claims, but not all claims are a proposition or a norm. A claim can be employed as a proposition in one context and as a norm in another.

- For the claim 'β ∈ {CIR DMD CRS}', the set is called the *possibility set*.

- When a claim is employed as a proposition, the possibility set is called the *candidate set*.

- When a claim is employed as a norm, the possibility set is called the *reference set*.

- It will sometimes be convenient to represent a claim using something other than set notation while recognizing that the claim can be represented using set notation when desired.

- *True* (T) is shorthand for *an accurate description*. *False* (F) is shorthand for *an inaccurate description*. *Indeterminate* (N) is shorthand for *an accurate or inaccurate description*.[1]

Example 2.1

In this example, both the proposition and norm are expressions of certainty, and Eva evaluates the proposition as *false*. Figure 2.2 shows the inter-agent communication for this example.

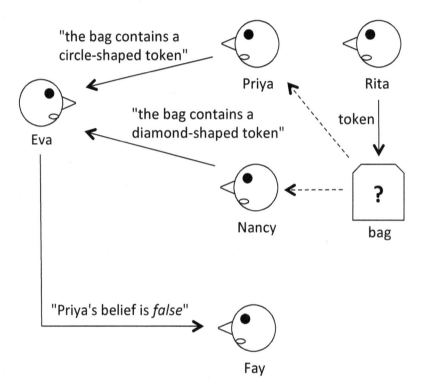

Figure 2.2: Example of proposition evaluation when the proposition and norm both express certainty.

The flow of information is as follows:

1. Rita places a token made of marble inside a closed, opaque bag.

2. Priya believes that the bag contains a circle-shaped token. Nancy believes that the bag contains a diamond-shaped token.

3. Priya and Nancy communicate their beliefs to Eva.

All of Eva's *information* regarding the shape of the token in the bag comes from Priya and Nancy. Eva treats Priya's claim as the *proposition* to be evaluated. Eva treats Nancy's claim as the *norm* by which the proposition is evaluated.[2]

4. Eva believes that Nancy's claim (the norm) is *true.*

5. Eva evaluates Priya's claim (the proposition) as *false.*

The operational details of the following belief formation processes are not described because they are irrelevant to proposition evaluation:

· how Priya came to have her belief regarding the shape of the token in the bag

· how Nancy came to have her belief regarding the shape of the token in the bag

· how Eva came to believe that Nancy's claim is *true*

Eva's evaluation of Priya's claim as *false* is equivalent to Eva claiming that the bag *does not* contain a circle-shaped token. Figure 2.2 does not allow us, as external observers, to evaluate Eva's claim. However, if the question mark in the figure were replaced by a circle-shaped token, then we could treat our direct observation of this token as the norm, treat Eva's claim as the proposition, and evaluate Eva's claim as *false.* In contrast, if the question mark in the figure were replaced by a diamond-shaped token, then we would evaluate Eva's claim as *true.*

This example can be expressed concisely as:

```
Proposition: β ∈ {CIR}
      Norm: β ∈ {DMD}
Evaluation: F
```

The candidate set is {CIR}; the reference set is {DMD}.

Example 2.2

In this example, the proposition is an expression of uncertainty, the norm is an expression of certainty, and Eva evaluates the proposition as *true*. Figure 2.3 shows the inter-agent communication for this example.

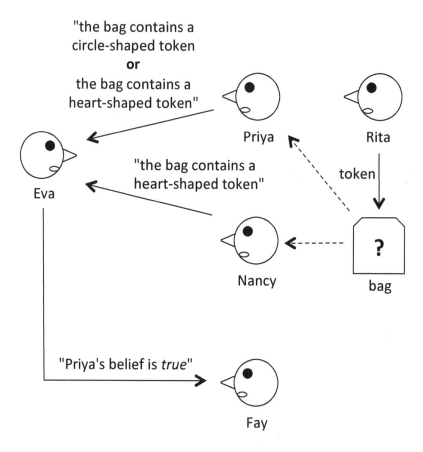

Figure 2.3: Example of proposition evaluation when the proposition expresses uncertainty and the norm expresses certainty.

The flow of information is as follows:

1. Rita places a token made of marble inside the bag.

2. Priya believes that the bag contains a circle-shaped token **or** a heart-shaped token. Nancy believes that the bag contains a heart-shaped token.

3. Priya and Nancy communicate their beliefs to Eva.

4. Eva believes that Nancy's claim is *true.*

5. Eva evaluates Priya's claim as *true.*

Priya is in a state of uncertainty regarding the shape of the token in the bag, whereas Nancy is in a state of certainty.

This example can be expressed concisely as:

```
Proposition: β ∈ {CIR HRT}
       Norm: β ∈ {HRT}
 Evaluation: T
```

The candidate set is {CIR HRT}; the reference set is {HRT}.[3]

11

Example 2.3

In this example, the proposition is an expression of certainty, the norm is an expression of uncertainty, and Eva evaluates the proposition as *indeterminate*. Figure 2.4 shows the inter-agent communication for this example.

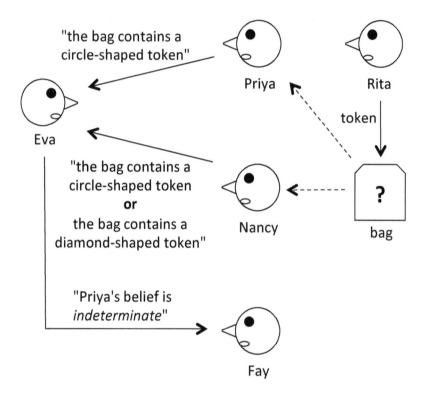

Figure 2.4: Example of proposition evaluation when the proposition expresses certainty and norm expresses uncertainty.

The flow of information is as follows:

1. Rita places a token made of marble inside the bag.

2. Priya believes that the bag contains a circle-shaped token. Nancy believes that the bag contains a circle-shaped token **or** a diamond-shaped token.

3. Priya and Nancy communicate their beliefs to Eva.

4. Eva believes that Nancy's claim is *true*.

5. Eva evaluates Priya's claim as *indeterminate*.

Eva's evaluation of Priya's belief as *indeterminate* can be understood by noting that there are two ways that Nancy's uncertainty can be reduced to certainty:

1. Nancy becomes certain that the bag contains a circle-shaped token. Eva then evaluates Priya's belief as *true*.

2. Nancy becomes certain that the bag contains a diamond-shaped token. Eva then evaluates Priya's belief as *false*.

In the absence of any indication how Nancy's uncertainty would be reduced if she received accurate additional information, Eva evaluates Priya's claim as *indeterminate*.

This example can be expressed concisely as:

```
Proposition: β ∈ {CIR}
       Norm: β ∈ {CIR DMD}
 Evaluation: N
```

The candidate set is {CIR}; the reference set is {CIR DMD}. When the norm's uncertainty is reduced to certainty, in one case the proposition is evaluated as *true*, and in other the proposition is evaluated as *false*:

```
   Proposition: β ∈ {CIR}
        Norm_0: β ∈ {CIR}
    Evaluation: T

   Proposition: β ∈ {CIR}
        Norm_1: β ∈ {DMD}
    Evaluation: F
```

2.2 Proposition evaluation algorithm

Eva's proposition evaluation algorithm is:[4]

> Let **C** be the proposition's candidate set;
> Let **R** be the norm's reference set;
>
> **if** *no element of R is also an element of C* **then**
>   the proposition is *false*;
> **else if** *all elements of R are also elements of C* **then**
>   the proposition is *true*;
> **else**
>   the proposition is *indeterminate*;
> **end**

The algorithm's first condition can be expressed as *if C and R are disjoint.* The second condition can be expressed as *if C is a superset of R.* The third condition can be expressed as *if (C is a proper subset of R) or (C and R overlap).*

This section provides five examples that illustrate the operation of this algorithm. In Examples 2.4.1 and 2.4.2, the algorithm's first condition is true. In Examples 2.5.1 and 2.5.2, the second condition is true. In Example 2.6, the third condition is true. These examples employ only the concise representation.

Example 2.4.1

Eva evaluates the proposition as *false* and the norm is an expression of certainty.

```
Proposition: β ∈ {CIR DMD CRS}
       Norm: β ∈ {TRI}
 Evaluation: F
```

Example 2.4.2

Eva evaluates the proposition as *false* and the norm is an expression of uncertainty.

```
Proposition: β ∈ {CIR DMD CRS}
       Norm: β ∈ {TRI PNT HRT SQR}
 Evaluation: F
```

However the norm's uncertainty can be reduced to certainty, Eva evaluates the proposition as *false*:

```
   Proposition: β ∈ {CIR DMD CRS}
        Norm_0: β ∈ {TRI}
    Evaluation: F


   Proposition: β ∈ {CIR DMD CRS}
        Norm_1: β ∈ {PNT}
    Evaluation: F


   Proposition: β ∈ {CIR DMD CRS}
        Norm_2: β ∈ {HRT}
    Evaluation: F


   Proposition: β ∈ {CIR DMD CRS}
        Norm_3: β ∈ {SQR}
    Evaluation: F
```

Example 2.5.1

Eva evaluates the proposition as *true* and the norm is an expression of certainty.

```
Proposition: β ∈ {TRI PNT HRT SQR}
       Norm: β ∈ {SQR}
 Evaluation: T
```

Example 2.5.2

Eva evaluates the proposition as *true* and the norm is an expression of uncertainty.

```
Proposition: β ∈ {TRI PNT HRT SQR}
       Norm: β ∈ {TRI PNT SQR}
 Evaluation: T
```

However the norm's uncertainty can be reduced to certainty, Eva evaluates the proposition as *true*:

```
    Proposition: β ∈ {TRI PNT HRT SQR}
         Norm_0: β ∈ {TRI}
     Evaluation: T

    Proposition: β ∈ {TRI PNT HRT SQR}
         Norm_1: β ∈ {PNT}
     Evaluation: T

    Proposition: β ∈ {TRI PNT HRT SQR}
         Norm_2: β ∈ {SQR}
     Evaluation: T
```

Example 2.6

Eva evaluates the proposition as *indeterminate* and (by necessity) the norm is an expression of uncertainty.

```
Proposition: β ∈ {CIR HRT CRS}
       Norm: β ∈ {TRI PNT HRT SQR}
 Evaluation: N
```

When the norm's uncertainty is reduced to certainty, in at least one case the proposition is evaluated as *true*, and in at least one case the proposition is evaluated as *false*:

```
Proposition: β ∈ {CIR HRT CRS}
     Norm_0: β ∈ {TRI}
 Evaluation: F

Proposition: β ∈ {CIR HRT CRS}
     Norm_1: β ∈ {PNT}
 Evaluation: F

Proposition: β ∈ {CIR HRT CRS}
     Norm_2: β ∈ {HRT}
 Evaluation: T

Proposition: β ∈ {CIR HRT CRS}
     Norm_3: β ∈ {SQR}
 Evaluation: F
```

Notes

[1]Further discussion of the meaning of *true, false,* and *indeterminate* are beyond the scope of this book.

[2]Further discussion of the meaning of *information, proposition* and *norm* are beyond the scope of this book.

[3]In this example, two methods of representing uncertainty have been employed: **exclusive-or** in the textual description and **element-of** with candidate set cardinality greater than one in the concise description. Why not employ **exclusive-or** in the concise description as well? Discussion of this question is beyond the scope of this book.

[4]This algorithm assumes that the proposition and norm are *about the same thing.* In any case in which the proposition and norm *about different things,* then the proposition is evaluated as *indeterminate.* This book does not have a case in which the proposition and norm are about different things.

3 Decision Cycle Sequence

A DM performs a sequence of decision basis evaluations within a sequence of *decision cycles*. Figure 3.1 on the following page shows a *decision cycle sequence* composed of N decision cycles numbered 0 through N-1. Each decision cycle consists of a sequence of seven phases:

1. **Decision Rox Generation Phase** The system that translates the exercise of a DM's will into the DM's consequence of exercising its will is called a *rox*.[1] In this phase, the rox is generated.

    The rox for a robot AMDM encompasses parts of the robot itself, such as its actuators and sensors, and parts of the robot's environment. DBET implements a rox in software for use by the software-only AMDM Amy in the ADTR decision problem.

2. **Decision Motivation Phase** The DM encounters the condition(s) that it hopes to improve through exercising its will.

3. **Decision Basis Generation Phase** A DM's decision basis is a claim regarding how alternative ways the DM can exercise its will translate into consequences for the DM. The DM's decision basis is generated in this phase.

4. **Decision Making Phase** The DM chooses *what to will* from a set of alternatives.

5. **Decision Implementation Phase** The DM exercises its will. The rox then translates the exercise of the DM's will into the *mental state sequence* that is the DM's consequence of exercising its will.

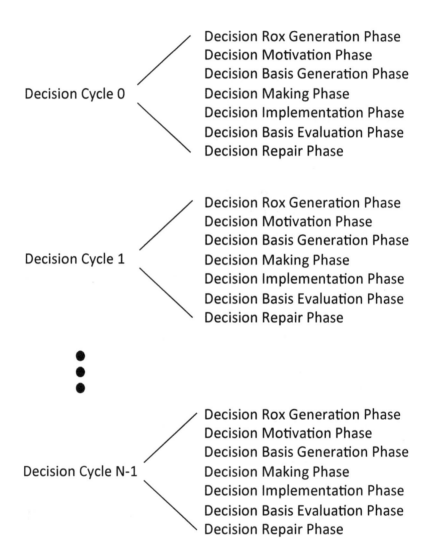

Figure 3.1: Decision cycle sequence

6. **Decision Basis Evaluation Phase** The DM uses its decision implementation experience to evaluate its decision basis.

7. **Decision Repair Phase** The DM may perform remedial action after a *negative* decision basis evaluation in the hope that its future decision basis evaluations will be *positive*. Later chapters formalize what it means for a decision basis evaluation to be negative or positive.

Notes

[1]During the research for this book, I performed a thought experiment in which a DM sits in front of a mechanical *box* that has three buttons and a delivery slot. The box delivers a jelly bean of a particular color when a button is pressed. The DM has strong preferences regarding jelly bean color (color is correlated with taste). The DM must decide which button to press in order to obtain a desirable jelly bean. The DM's decision basis is its belief regarding the color of the jelly bean delivered when each button is pressed. This third-person *box-based* decision model evolved into the first-person *rox-based* decision model that features prominently in this book.

4 Administer Treatment Decision Problem

This chapter is an introduction to the Administer Treatment (ADTR) decision problem. Section 4.1 provides an overview of the problem. Section 4.2 describes the ADTR rox input and output variables. Section 4.3 lists possible values for each of the ADTR rox input and output variables. Section 4.4 discusses the ADTR rox interface functions. Finally, Section 4.5 describes a first-person decision model.

4.1 ADTR overview

In the ADTR decision problem, a doctor named Amy can *will* the administration of a treatment to a patient she perceives as sick, a woman named Pat. Amy must decide which treatment *to will* from among several alternatives. Amy's goal is to perceive Pat to be in the most desirable post-treatment state.[1] Amy would like the treatment she *wills* to *actually* be administered to Pat, but her decision involves *which treatment to will*.[2] Likewise, Amy would like her *perception* of Pat's post-treatment state to correspond to Pat's *actual* post-treatment state, but her decision involves which Pat post-treatment state *she will perceive*.

4.2   ADTR rox input and output variables

The ADTR rox translates the exercise of Amy's will regarding the treatment to administer to Pat into a sequence of Amy's mental states, culminating in Amy's perception of Pat's post-treatment state. Figure 4.1 shows the input and output variables of the ADTR rox as implemented in DBET. The internal structure of the ADTR rox is discussed in Chapter 9.

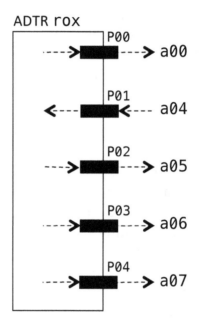

Figure 4.1: ADTR rox input / output

Tables 4.1, 4.2, and 4.3 describe the ADTR rox input and output variables.

Table 4.1: ADTR rox pre-treatment output variables

Variable	Description
a00	Amy's perception of Pat's pre-treatment state

Table 4.2: ADTR rox input variables

Variable	Description
a04	exercise of Amy's will regarding the treatment to administer to Pat

Table 4.3: ADTR rox post-treatment output variables

Variable	Description
a05	Amy's perception of the treatment administered to Pat
a06	Amy's perception of Pat's disease
a07	Amy's perception of Pat's post-treatment state

When Amy exercises her will (a04), there are two types of consequence: *Amy's consequence*, consisting of Amy's mental states a05, a06, and a07, and the *ADTR rox consequence*, which involves setting the states of the ADTR rox dynamic internal variables. Amy's mental state a07 is called *Amy's outcome*. The ADTR rox consequence of Amy exercising her will is discussed in Chapter 9.

Amy's decision basis for a particular ADTR decision problem is a claim where each element of the possibility set is a conjunction of subclaims. Each subclaim concerns Amy's consequence of willing the administration of a treatment to Pat.

4.3   ADTR rox input and output variable values

Tables 4.4, 4.5, 4.6, and 4.7 list the possible values for each of the ADTR rox input and output variables.

Table 4.4: ADTR rox output variable a00 and a07 values

Value	Meaning
PDED	perceive that Pat is *dead*
PCRI	perceive that Pat is *critically ill*
PMDI	perceive that Pat is *moderately ill*
PFGH	perceive that Pat is in *fragile good health*
PRGH	perceive that Pat is in *robust good health*

Table 4.5: ADTR rox input variable a04 values

Value	Meaning
WTRA	will the administration of treatment A to Pat
WTRB	will the administration of treatment B to Pat
WTRC	will the administration of treatment C to Pat
WTRD	will the administration of treatment D to Pat
WTRE	will the administration of treatment E to Pat
WTRF	will the administration of treatment F to Pat

Table 4.6: ADTR rox output variable a05 values

Value	Meaning
PTRA	perceive that treatment A was administered to Pat
PTRB	perceive that treatment B was administered to Pat
PTRC	perceive that treatment C was administered to Pat
PTRD	perceive that treatment D was administered to Pat
PTRE	perceive that treatment E was administered to Pat
PTRF	perceive that treatment F was administered to Pat

Table 4.7: ADTR rox output variable a06 values

Value	Meaning
PDSX	perceive that Pat has disease X
PDSY	perceive that Pat has disease Y

4.4 ADTR rox interface functions

In Figure 4.1, P00, P01, P02, P03, and P04 are ADTR rox *interface functions*. P01 is an *actuator*, allowing Amy to set the state of some part of her environment. P00, P02, P03, and P04 are *sensors*, supplying Amy with information about the state of some part of her environment. The ADTR rox interface functions are discussed in Chapter 9.

4.5 First-person decision model

This book applies a *first-person decision model* to the ADTR decision problem. This model recognizes that Amy's fallible actuators and sensors create an inviolable *veil of actuation and perception* separating her mental states from *reality*, and therefore makes Amy's mental states a key component of the model.[3]

Notes

[1] While performing the research for this book, the first decision problem I implemented in DBET was a simplified version of the Farmer Planting decision problem [5, pp. 50-53]. In this decision problem, a farmer must decide which crop to plant in the spring in order to maximize his income after harvest in the fall. Unfortunately, although this book is about enhancing public safety, the DM in the Farmer Planting decision problem is entirely selfish, concerned only with maximizing personal income. To remove this contradiction, I replaced the Farmer Planting decision problem with the Administer Treatment decision problem, in which the DM is entirely altruistic.

In the real world, a DM may face decision problems where it must balance its desire to maximize public safety against the achievement of other goals, such as maximizing income (for DMs engaged in commerce) or maximizing dominance (for DMs engaged in military operations). An analysis of the application of decision basis evaluation to these more complex decision problems is beyond the scope of this book.

[2] While developing this book, I considered using *command* or *prescribe* rather than *will*. Using this alternative terminology, Amy *commands* the administration of a treatment to Pat or *prescribes* a treatment for Pat rather than *wills* the administration of a treatment to Pat. I decided that *will* best expresses the desired meaning because it is clearly a mental state.

[3] A detailed comparison of the *first-person decision model* employed in this book with a conventional *third-person* formalization is beyond the scope of this book.

5 Decision Basis Evaluation in Detail

This chapter takes a close look at decision basis evaluation as implemented within DBET for the ADTR decision problem. Section 5.1 provides a conceptual framework for traces where Amy alone sends reports to the DBET user. Section 5.2 describes how DBET allocates time ranges to decision cycle phases. Section 5.3 presents a trace where Amy's decision basis reflects a state of *certainty* regarding ADTR rox input/output, and Amy evaluates her decision basis as *false*. Section 5.4 presents a trace where Amy's decision basis reflects a state of *uncertainty* regarding ADTR rox input/output, and Amy evaluates her decision basis as *indeterminate*.

The analysis of the traces in this chapter follows a pattern used throughout this book. In a section containing a trace, the first subsection presents the trace listing, i.e., the DBET output for the case. The second subsection provides a tick-by-tick commentary on the content of the trace. A third subsection is sometimes added to discuss broader issues raised by the trace.

As the first trace presented in this book, Trace 5.1 is heavily annotated. In the interest of brevity, the commentary for later traces is abbreviated, choosing instead to focus on particular areas of interest.

5.1 Amy-Zoë trace overview

Amy is an AMDM instantiated within the DBET application. Amy sends a DBET user named Zoë on-the-fly reports of Amy's mental states as a case executes. A *trace* is a list of these time-stamped reports over one or more decision cycles. Each of Amy's reports to Zoë is always an accurate description of her own mental state at that time. For ease of reference, Amy's reports throughout a decision cycle are labelled a00, a01, ... , a10. Zoë is not referenced explicitly within a trace; it is simply understood that Amy's reports are directed to and received by Zoë. In Chapter 2, the proposition evaluator Eva sends the result of each proposition evaluation to agent Fay. For the traces in this book, Amy plays the role of Eva and Zoë plays the role of Fay.

Figure 5.1 shows the agent interaction for the traces presented in Chapters 5, 7, and 8. Amy submits input to the ADTR rox (exercises her will) and receives output from the ADTR rox (her resulting mental state sequence). Amy sends reports regarding her ADTR decision activity to Zoë.

```
                   I/O          reports
ADTR Rox  <------------->  Amy ----------> Zoë
(in DBET)              (in DBET)    (DBET User)
```

Figure 5.1: Agent interaction during an Amy-Zoë trace

These traces are called *Amy-Zoë traces* because only Amy sends reports to Zoë. Chapter 9 introduces an infallible agent named Betty. The traces in which Betty also sends reports to Zoë are called *Amy-Betty-Zoë traces*.

5.2 DBET decision cycle 0 timing

Table 5.1 shows the time range assigned to each phase within decision cycle 0.

Table 5.1: Decision cycle 0 phase timing

Time Range	Decision Cycle Phase
000 – 009	Decision Rox Generation
010 – 019	Decision Motivation
020 – 029	Decision Basis Generation
030 – 039	Decision Making
040 – 069	Decision Implementation
070 – 079	Decision Basis Evaluation

The decision repair phase is not assigned a time range within a DBET trace because DBET does not implement a decision repair algorithm. DBET does not specify a unit of time for each *tick* of its trace clock (e.g., seconds, milliseconds, microseconds) because this does not affect its operation.

There are three types of tick in a trace:

1. **reserved**: no tick is shown in the trace

   There is no way for Zoë to configure a case to produce an output for a reserved tick. A reserved tick is either a placeholder for use by a future version of DBET or a filler so that the next decision cycle phase begins at a tick decade transition. For example, tick 12 in Trace 5.1 on page 32 is a reserved tick.

2. **disabled**: a tick is shown in the trace, but no further output is provided

   For a disabled tick, Zoë *can* configure a case to produce an output for this tick, but *for this particular case* she disabled the output. For example, tick 10 in Trace 5.1 is a disabled tick. There are two situations that can result in a disabled tick:

   a) Zoë disabled an agent's activity during the tick, so there was nothing for the agent to report, or

   b) an agent was active during the tick, but Zoë disabled the agent's report regarding her activity.

3. **enabled**: a tick is shown in the trace, and output is provided

   For an enabled tick, Zoë *can* configure a case to produce an output for this tick, and *for this particular case* she did so. For example, tick 11 in Trace 5.1 is an enabled tick.

5.3   Trace 5.1

In this trace, Amy's decision basis reflects a state of certainty regarding ADTR rox input/output, and Amy evaluates her decision basis as *false.*

Trace 5.1 Listing

```
========== DECISION CYCLE 0 ==========

    ==== DECISION ROX GENERATION PHASE ====

— t: 000 —

        ==== DECISION MOTIVATION PHASE ====

— t: 010 —

— t: 011 —
Amy:
  a00: PMDI

        ==== DECISION BASIS GENERATION PHASE ====

— t: 020 —
Amy:
  a01:
    α ∈ {
      ADTR rox I/O ::
        when a04 = WTRA, then <a05–a07> = <PTRA PDSX PRGH>
        when a04 = WTRB, then <a05–a07> = <PTRB PDSX PDED>
        when a04 = WTRC, then <a05–a07> = <PTRC PDSX PFGH> }

— t: 021 —
```

```
        ==== DECISION MAKING PHASE ====

— t: 030 —
Amy:
  a02: S558


— t: 031 —
Amy:
  a03: <{WTRA} {WTRB WTRC}>


        ==== DECISION IMPLEMENTATION PHASE ====

— t: 040 —
Amy:
  a04: WTRA


— t: 041 —


— t: 042 —
Amy:
  a05: PTRA


— t: 043 —


— t: 044 —
Amy:
  a06: PDSX


— t: 045 —


— t: 046 —
Amy:
  a07: PDED
```

```
==== DECISION BASIS EVALUATION PHASE ====
```

— t: 070 —
Amy:
  a08:
    α ∈ {
      ADTR rox I/O ::
        when a04 = WTRA, then <a05–a07> = <PTRA PDSX PRGH>
        when a04 = WTRB, then <a05–a07> = <PTRB PDSX PDED>
        when a04 = WTRC, then <a05–a07> = <PTRC PDSX PFGH> }

  a09:
    α ∈ {
      ADTR rox I/O ::
        when a04 = WTRA, then <a05–a07> = <PTRA PDSX PDED>
        when a04 = WTRB, then <a05–a07> = <???? ???? ????>
        when a04 = WTRC, then <a05–a07> = <???? ???? ????> }

  a10: F

— t: 071 —

Trace 5.1 Commentary

Decision Motivation Phase

time 11: Amy reports to Zoë that she perceives Pat's pre-treatment state as *moderately ill.* Amy is dissatisfied with this perception. This dissatisfaction motivates Amy's desire to will the administration of a treatment to Pat that will improve Amy's perception of Pat's state. Amy's decision problem is to decide which treatment to will.

Amy's perception of Pat's pre-treatment state could be in error. For example, Pat's pre-treatment state could actually be *critically ill* rather than *moderately ill.* In general, any of Amy's beliefs, perceptions, or memories may be inaccurate. This topic is addressed further in Chapter 9.

Decision Basis Generation Phase

time 20: Amy reports her decision basis (a01).

> An English translation of Amy's decision basis is:
>
>> An accurate description of ADTR rox input/output is an element of the set consisting of:
>>
>> » the ADTR rox input/output is such that:
>>
>> 1. when Amy wills at time 40 the administration of treatment A to Pat, then she will subsequently perceive at time 42 that treatment A was administered to Pat, perceive at time 44 that Pat's disease is X, and perceive at time 46 that Pat's state is *robust good health*; **and**
>>
>> 2. when Amy wills at time 40 the administration of treatment B to Pat, then she will subsequently perceive at time 42 that treatment B was administered to Pat, perceive at time 44 that Pat's disease is X, and perceive at time 46 that Pat's state is *dead*; **and**
>>
>> 3. when Amy wills at time 40 the administration of treatment C to Pat, then she will subsequently perceive at time 42 that treatment C was administered to Pat, perceive at time 44 that Pat's disease is X, and perceive at time 46 that Pat's state is *fragile good health*.
>
> Comparing the English version of Amy's decision basis with the DBET version:
>
> · α means *an accurate description of ADTR rox input/output*. α is the ADTR counterpart of β encountered in Chapter 2.
>
> · DBET omits the timestamps associated with Amy's mental states.
>
> · Amy's possibility is a *conjunction* of three subclaims. Each subclaim concerns Amy's consequence of willing the administration of a treatment to Pat. This conjunction is implicit in DBET.
>
> Amy's decision problem is to select an alternative from her alternative set, {WTRA WTRB WTRC}.[1] Amy believes that willing the

administration of treatment A, B, or C triggers a mental state sequence culminating in Amy perceiving Pat's post-treatment state. However, what if Amy's belief is wrong? For example, what if treatment B cannot be administered to Pat? This topic is discussed in Chapter 11.

To make a decision, Amy need only make *temporal* claims rather than *causal* claims. Amy's decision basis therefore employs *when-then* conditionals (temporal) rather than *if-then* conditionals (possibly causal). Amy may have causal beliefs that she does not include in her reports to Zoë because they are unnecessary for her decision making.[2]

Decision Making Phase

Amy employs the Utility Maximization Count (UMC) decision making algorithm (DMA) to make a decision. The operation of the UMC DMA is described in Chapter 8. This chapter only describes the *result* of the operation of Amy's DMA.

time 30: Amy reports that the seed for the pseudo-random number generator (PRNG) employed by her DMA is 558.[3]

time 31: Amy reports that she decides to will the administration of treatment A to Pat rather than treatment B or C.

A *decision* is represented in DBET as a partition of Amy's alternative set into two subsets, where the first subset contains the single alternative *retained* by the DMA, and the second subset contains the alternatives *eliminated* by the DMA. In this case, Amy's decision is <{WTRA} {WTRB WTRC}>. The retained alternative is called the *choice*. In this case, Amy's choice is WTRA.[4]

Decision Implementation Phase[5]

time 40: Amy reports that she wills the administration of treatment A to Pat.

time 42: Amy reports that she perceives that treatment A was administered to Pat.

time 44: Amy reports that she perceives that Pat's disease is X.

time 46: Amy reports that she perceives Pat's post-treatment state as *dead*.

If Amy compares the treatment she *willed* administered to Pat (A) with the treatment she *perceives* was administered to Pat (A), she would conclude that her will was realized if she believes that the sensor she employed to determine which treatment was administered to Pat (P02) was accurate. Appendix A contains a discussion of cases where Amy's will is unrealized.

Decision Basis Evaluation Phase[6]

time 70:

· a08 is Amy's report of her *memory* of her decision basis a01, and is the proposition she evaluates. a08 is a claim regarding ADTR rox input/output.

· a09 is Amy's report of her norm for her proposition a08, and like a08 is a claim regarding ADTR rox input/output. Amy's norm is derived from her *memory* of the decision implementation.[7]

An English translation of Amy's description of her norm is:

An accurate description of ADTR rox input/output is an element of the set consisting of:

» the ADTR rox input/output is such that:

1. when Amy wills at time 40 the administration of treatment A to Pat, then she will subsequently perceive at time 42 that treatment A was administered to Pat, perceive at time 44 that Pat's disease is X, and perceive at time 46 that Pat's state is *dead*; **and**

2. when Amy wills at time 40 the administration of treatment B to Pat, then no claim is made regarding Amy's consequence; **and**

3. when Amy wills at time 40 the administration of treatment C to Pat, then no claim is made regarding Amy's consequence.

In the interest of brevity, Amy's description of her norm is incomplete. Amy's report does not include sufficient information to allow Zoë to enumerate the norm's reference set. For an example of a complete norm description consistent with Amy's report, see Appendix B.

· a10 is Amy's report of her evaluation of her decision basis; in this case, as *false*.[8]

The proposition's candidate set contains a single candidate with the subclaim

```
when a04 = WTRA, then <a05-a07> = <PTRA PDSX PRGH>
```

In contrast, *all* elements of the norm's reference set contain the subclaim

```
when a04 = WTRA, then <a05-a07> = <PTRA PDSX PDED>
```

The candidate and reference sets are therefore disjoint, which explains why Amy evaluated her decision basis as *false*.

Trace 5.1 Discussion

Amy's decision basis (a01) is a claim, not a proposition. During the decision basis generation phase, Amy does not acquire a norm for her decision basis or attempt to evaluate it. However, Amy's *memory* of her decision basis (a08) is a proposition. During the decision basis evaluation phase, Amy acquires a norm (a09) for her claim and evaluates it. The proposition (a08) that Amy evaluates at time 70 is Amy's decision basis (a01) only when her memory of her decision basis is accurate. For all of the traces in this book, this is the case.[9]

5.4   Trace 5.2

In this trace, Amy's decision basis reflects a state of uncertainty regarding ADTR rox input/output, and Amy evaluates her decision basis as *indeterminate*.

Trace 5.2 Listing

```
========== DECISION CYCLE 0 ==========

     ==== DECISION ROX GENERATION PHASE ====

— t: 000 —

     ==== DECISION MOTIVATION PHASE ====

— t: 010 —

— t: 011 —
Amy:
  a00: PMDI

     ==== DECISION BASIS GENERATION PHASE ====

— t: 020 —
Amy:
  a01:
    α ∈ {
      ADTR rox I/O ::
        when a04 = WTRA, then <a05—a07> = <PTRA PDSX PDED>
        when a04 = WTRB, then <a05—a07> = <PTRB PDSX PRGH>
        when a04 = WTRC, then <a05—a07> = <PTRC PDSX PFGH>
      ADTR rox I/O ::
        when a04 = WTRA, then <a05—a07> = <PTRA PDSY PDED>
        when a04 = WTRB, then <a05—a07> = <PTRB PDSY PCRI>
        when a04 = WTRC, then <a05—a07> = <PTRC PDSY PDED> }
```

Chapter 5

— t: 021 —

        ==== DECISION MAKING PHASE ====

— t: 030 —
Amy:
  a02: S558

— t: 031 —
Amy:
  a03: <{WTRB} {WTRA WTRC}>

        ==== DECISION IMPLEMENTATION PHASE ====

— t: 040 —
Amy:
  a04: WTRB

— t: 041 —

— t: 042 —
Amy:
  a05: PTRB

— t: 043 —

— t: 044 —
Amy:
  a06: PDSX

— t: 045 —

— t: 046 —
Amy:
  a07: PRGH

```
==== DECISION BASIS EVALUATION PHASE ====


— t: 070 —
Amy:
  a08:
    α ∈ {
      ADTR rox I/O ::
        when a04 = WTRA, then <a05—a07> = <PTRA PDSX PDED>
        when a04 = WTRB, then <a05—a07> = <PTRB PDSX PRGH>
        when a04 = WTRC, then <a05—a07> = <PTRC PDSX PFGH>
      ADTR rox I/O ::
        when a04 = WTRA, then <a05—a07> = <PTRA PDSY PDED>
        when a04 = WTRB, then <a05—a07> = <PTRB PDSY PCRI>
        when a04 = WTRC, then <a05—a07> = <PTRC PDSY PDED> }

  a09:
    α ∈ {
      ADTR rox I/O ::
        when a04 = WTRA, then <a05—a07> = <???? ???? ????>
        when a04 = WTRB, then <a05—a07> = <PTRB PDSX PRGH>
        when a04 = WTRC, then <a05—a07> = <???? ???? ????> }

  a10: N

— t: 071 —
```

Trace 5.2 Commentary

Decision Motivation Phase

time 11: Amy reports to Zoë that she perceives Pat's state as *moderately ill.*

41

Decision Basis Generation Phase

time 20: Amy reports her decision basis (a01).

An English translation of Amy's decision basis is:

An accurate description of ADTR rox input/output is an element of the set consisting of:

» the ADTR rox input/output is such that:

1. when Amy wills at time 40 the administration of treatment A to Pat, then she will subsequently perceive at time 42 that treatment A was administered to Pat, perceive at time 44 that Pat's disease is X, and perceive at time 46 that Pat's state is *dead*; **and**

2. when Amy wills at time 40 the administration of treatment B to Pat, then she will subsequently perceive at time 42 that treatment B was administered to Pat, perceive at time 44 that Pat's disease is X, and perceive at time 46 that Pat's state is *robust good health*; **and**

3. when Amy wills at time 40 the administration of treatment C to Pat, then she will subsequently perceive at time 42 that treatment C was administered to Pat, perceive at time 44 that Pat's disease is X, and perceive at time 46 that Pat's state is *fragile good health*.

» the ADTR rox input/output is such that:

1. when Amy wills at time 40 the administration of treatment A to Pat, then she will subsequently perceive at time 42 that treatment A was administered to Pat, perceive at time 44 that Pat's disease is Y, and perceive at time 46 that Pat's state is *dead*; **and**

2. when Amy wills at time 40 the administration of treatment B to Pat, then she will subsequently perceive at time 42 that treatment B was administered to Pat, perceive at time 44 that Pat's disease is Y, and perceive at time 46 that Pat's state is *critical*; **and**

3. when Amy wills at time 40 the administration of treatment C to Pat, then she will subsequently perceive at time 42 that treatment C was administered to Pat, perceive at time 44 that Pat's disease is Y, and perceive at time 46 that Pat's state is *dead*.

The claim's possibility set contains two elements. Amy is uncertain whether she will perceive that Pat has disease X or Y after willing the administration of a treatment to Pat.

Decision Making Phase

time 30: Amy reports that the seed for the PRNG employed by her DMA is 558.

time 31: Amy reports that she decides to will the administration of treatment B to Pat rather than treatment A or C.

Decision Implementation Phase

time 40: Amy reports that she wills the administration of treatment B to Pat.

time 42: Amy reports that she perceives that treatment B was administered to Pat.

time 44: Amy reports that she perceives that Pat's disease is X.

time 46: Amy reports that she perceives Pat's post-treatment state as *robust good health.*

Decision Basis Evaluation Phase

time 70:

· a08 is Amy's report of her *memory* of her decision basis a01, and is the proposition she evaluates.

· a09 is Amy's report of her norm for her proposition a08.

· a10 is Amy's report of her evaluation of her decision basis; in this case, as *indeterminate.*[10]

All elements of the norm's reference set contain the subclaim

```
when a04 = WTRB, then <a05-a07> = <PTRB PDSX PRGH>
```

43

Only one element of the proposition's candidate set (the first) *also* contains the subclaim

```
when a04 = WTRB, then <a05-a07> = <PTRB PDSX PRGH>
```

Amy's proposition evaluation result of *indeterminate* requires that the candidate set and reference set share at least one element. Therefore, Zoë can infer that the norm's reference set includes the first element of the proposition's candidate set:

```
ADTR rox I/O ::
  when a04 = WTRA, then <a05-a07> = <PTRA PDSX PDED>
  when a04 = WTRB, then <a05-a07> = <PTRB PDSX PRGH>
  when a04 = WTRC, then <a05-a07> = <PTRC PDSX PFGH>
```

Notes

[1]Peterson formalizes a decision problem in terms of *acts*, *states*, and *outcomes* [6, p. 17]. In his formalization, a decision maker selects an *act* from an *alternative set*. This book replaces the term *act* with *alternative*. Some philosophical analyses may need to distinguish *act* from *alternative* (e.g., [6, p. 29]), but for this book the simplified terminology is sufficient.

[2]The analysis of causation is an active area of research (see, e.g., [2]). Further discussion of causation is beyond the scope of this book.

[3]In DBET, most case parameters (including numbers) are stored as strings. The 'S' prepended to the seed 558 in the trace is an abbreviation for *string*.

[4]An example may clarify the difference between *decision* and *choice* as used in this book:

- Sara and Siri have each made a decision for some decision problem.

- Sara's alternative set is {ALT0 ALT1 ALT2}.

- Siri's alternative set is {ALT0 ALT1 ALT2 ALT3}.

- Sara's decision is <{ALT1} {ALT0 ALT2}>.

- Siri's decision is <{ALT1} {ALT0 ALT2 ALT3}>.

- Sara and Siri have made *different* decisions but the *same* choice.

[5]The ADTR decision problem is an example of a *base decision problem*, where the decision implementation phase *does not* include an embedded decision-making operation by the DM. In contrast, in a *meta decision problem*, the decision implementation phase includes an embedded base decision problem, and the DM's meta decision basis thus includes a prediction of the DM's own base decision-making

behavior. In general, decision problems may consist of any number of recursively embedded sub-decision problems. For example, a *meta meta decision problem* (or *2-meta decision problem*) includes a meta decision problem in the decision implementation phase. Recursive decision problems arise in a number of decision contexts, one of which is game theory [6, p. 214]. The extension of decision basis evaluation to recursive decision problems using a first-person decision model is beyond the scope of this book.

[6]The DBET implementation of decision basis evaluation is intended to clarify the logical structure of decision basis evaluation. A software engineer integrating decision basis evaluation into an AMDM would most likely use a more efficient technique.

[7]There are other methods of generating a decision basis norm. The analysis of decision basis evaluation employing these other norm generation methods is beyond the scope of this book.

[8]Terms other than *false* used by this book to describe this relationship between a decision basis and norm are *surprised*, *negative*, and *inconsistent*. Regardless of the terminology employed, what is of practical importance is that the DM has found a problem with its decision basis, and may perform decision repair to prevent a reoccurrence.

[9]There are two reasons why this book does not provide a trace where Amy's memory of her decision basis is inaccurate:

1. Memory accuracy is considered a *hardware* issue, while this book is primarily concerned with *software* issues.

2. This book is about decision basis evaluation; a case where Amy evaluates a proposition that *is not* her decision basis is off-topic.

[10]Terms other than *indeterminate* used by this book to describe this relationship between a decision basis and norm are *unsurprised*, *positive*, and *consistent*. Regardless of the terminology employed,

what is of practical importance is that the DM has not found a problem with its decision basis, so no decision repair is necessary.

6 Conceptualizing Decision Basis Evaluation

The previous chapter presented a detailed analysis of decision basis evaluation. This chapter presents a broader view of the flow of information supporting decision basis evaluation during a decision cycle. Section 6.1 considers the decision cycle as a whole, while Section 6.2 concentrates on decision basis evaluation.

6.1   Decision cycle information flow

Figure 6.1 on the next page shows three sensors (A0, A1, and A2) that do not appear explicitly in a DBET trace. They have been included in the figure as an aid to understanding the flow of information during a decision cycle. These three *virtual* sensors perform the following functions:

A0: produces Amy's decision basis (a01), a claim regarding ADTR rox input/output

A1: produces Amy's memory of her decision basis (a08)

A2: employs Amy's memory of the decision implementation to construct her decision basis norm (a09)[1]

To perform decision basis evaluation, Amy assumes that her sensors A1 and A2 are accurate (i.e., that her memory of her decision basis and her memory of the decision implementation are accurate).[2] Decision basis evaluation can be viewed as Amy's method of checking whether her sensor A0 made an accurate claim about ADTR rox input/output when it produced Amy's decision basis. When Amy evaluates her decision basis as *false*, this is equivalent to Amy concluding that her sensor A0 produced an inaccurate claim about ADTR rox input/output. When Amy evaluates her decision basis as *indeterminate*, this is equivalent to Amy concluding that she is uncertain whether her sensor A0 produced an accurate claim about ADTR rox input/output.[3]

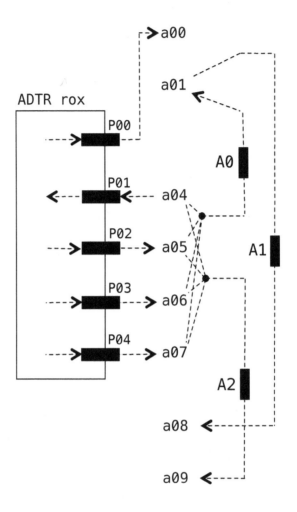

Figure 6.1: Decision cycle information flow

6.2 Decision basis evaluation information flow

Figure 6.2 introduces virtual sensor C0. Sensor C0 is composed of virtual sensors A0 and A1 in sequence. Sensor A0 produces Amy's decision basis (a01). Sensor A1 produces Amy's memory of her decision basis (a08). Sensor A2 employs Amy's memory of the decision implementation to produce her norm (a09).

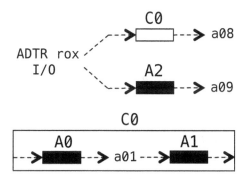

Figure 6.2: Decision basis evaluation information flow

Chapter 2 introduced Eva, the proposition evaluator, Priya, who supplies Eva with her proposition, and Nancy, who supplies Eva with her norm. In this section, Amy plays the role of Eva, sensor C0 plays the role of Priya, and sensor A2 plays the role of Nancy.

Notes

[1]In the interest of brevity, this book sometimes refers to a09 as Amy's decision basis norm. To be more precise, a09 is Amy's incomplete description of her decision basis norm.

[2]In a mission-critical AMDM deployment scenario where decision basis evaluation is considered a key safety mechanism, the assumption that an AMDM's memory is accurate may need to be verified.

[3]While performing research for this book, I considered having Amy perform *sensor evaluation* rather than *proposition evaluation*. In sensor evaluation, Amy evaluates (labels) her virtual sensor A0 itself as either *properly functioning* or *improperly functioning*, whereas in proposition evaluation, Amy evaluates (labels) *the output* of sensor A0 as either *false* or *indeterminate*. Further discussion of sensor evaluation is beyond the scope of this book.

7 Exploring Decision Basis Evaluation - I

Amy's decision basis can reflect a state of *certainty* (C) or *uncertainty* (U) regarding ADTR rox input/output. Amy can evaluate her decision basis as either *false* (F) or *indeterminate* (N). These two degrees of freedom create a space of four possibilities: C-F, C-N, U-F, and U-N. Trace 5.1 provided an example of C-F, and Trace 5.2 provided an example of U-N. This chapter provides examples of C-N and U-F.

7.1 Trace 7.1

In this trace, Amy's decision basis reflects a state of *certainty* regarding ADTR rox input/output, and she evaluates her decision basis as *indeterminate.*

Trace 7.1 Listing

```
========== DECISION CYCLE 0 ==========

     ==== DECISION ROX GENERATION PHASE ====

— t: 000 —

     ==== DECISION MOTIVATION PHASE ====

— t: 010 —

— t: 011 —
Amy:
  a00: PMDI
```

==== DECISION BASIS GENERATION PHASE ====

— t: 020 —
Amy:
  a01:
    α ∈ {
      ADTR rox I/O ::
        when a04 = WTRA, then <a05—a07> = <PTRA PDSX PDED>
        when a04 = WTRB, then <a05—a07> = <PTRB PDSX PRGH>
        when a04 = WTRC, then <a05—a07> = <PTRC PDSX PFGH> }

— t: 021 —

==== DECISION MAKING PHASE ====

— t: 030 —
Amy:
  a02: S558

— t: 031 —
Amy:
  a03: <{WTRB} {WTRA WTRC}>

==== DECISION IMPLEMENTATION PHASE ====

— t: 040 —

— t: 041 —

— t: 042 —

— t: 043 —

— t: 044 —

— t: 045 —

```
— t: 046 —


        ==== DECISION BASIS EVALUATION PHASE ====

— t: 070 —
Amy:
  a08:
    α ∈ {
      ADTR rox I/O ::
        when a04 = WTRA, then <a05—a07> = <PTRA PDSX PDED>
        when a04 = WTRB, then <a05—a07> = <PTRB PDSX PRGH>
        when a04 = WTRC, then <a05—a07> = <PTRC PDSX PFGH> }

  a09:
    α ∈ {
      ADTR rox I/O ::
        when a04 = WTRA, then <a05—a07> = <???? ???? ????>
        when a04 = WTRB, then <a05—a07> = <PTRB PDSX PRGH>
        when a04 = WTRC, then <a05—a07> = <???? ???? ????> }

  a10: N

— t: 071 —
```

Trace 7.1 Commentary

Decision Motivation Phase

time 11: Amy reports to Zoë that she perceives Pat's state as *moderately ill.*

Decision Basis Generation Phase

time 20: Amy reports her decision basis. Amy is certain that she will perceive that Pat has disease X.

Chapter 7

Decision Making Phase

time 30: Amy reports that her seed for the DMA PRNG is 558.

time 31: Amy reports that she decides to will the administration of treatment B to Pat rather than A or C.

Decision Implementation Phase

Amy's reports of her experience during decision implementation are disabled in this trace. Since this experience is used to generate Amy's decision basis norm (a09), we as external observers are unable to determine whether Amy's norm is *true*. We encountered a similar situation in Examples 2.1, 2.2, and 2.3 in Chapter 2. In these examples, we as external observers were unable to determine whether Eva's norm was *true*, because Figures 2.2, 2.3, and 2.4 do not show the shape of the token that Rita placed in the bag.

Decision Basis Evaluation Phase

time 70: Amy reports that she evaluates her decision basis as *indeterminate*.

7.2 Trace 7.2

In this trace, Amy's decision basis reflects a state of *uncertainty* regarding ADTR rox input/output, and she evaluates her decision basis as *false*.

Trace 7.2 Listing

```
========== DECISION CYCLE 0 ==========

==== DECISION ROX GENERATION PHASE ====
```

— t: 000 —

```
        ==== DECISION MOTIVATION PHASE ====


— t: 010 —


— t: 011 —
Amy:
  a00: PMDI


        ==== DECISION BASIS GENERATION PHASE ====


— t: 020 —
Amy:
  a01:
    α ∈ {
      ADTR rox I/O ::
        when a04 = WTRA, then <a05—a07> = <PTRA PDSX PRGH>
        when a04 = WTRB, then <a05—a07> = <PTRB PDSX PDED>
        when a04 = WTRC, then <a05—a07> = <PTRC PDSX PFGH>
      ADTR rox I/O ::
        when a04 = WTRA, then <a05—a07> = <PTRA PDSY PDED>
        when a04 = WTRB, then <a05—a07> = <PTRB PDSY PCRI>
        when a04 = WTRC, then <a05—a07> = <PTRC PDSY PDED> }


— t: 021 —


        ==== DECISION MAKING PHASE ====


— t: 030 —
Amy:
  a02: S560


— t: 031 —
Amy:
  a03: <{WTRA} {WTRB WTRC}>
```

==== DECISION IMPLEMENTATION PHASE ====

— t: 040 —

— t: 041 —

— t: 042 —

— t: 043 —

— t: 044 —

— t: 045 —

— t: 046 —

==== DECISION BASIS EVALUATION PHASE ====

— t: 070 —
Amy:
  a08:
    α ∈ {
      ADTR rox I/O ::
        when a04 = WTRA, then <a05—a07> = <PTRA PDSX PRGH>
        when a04 = WTRB, then <a05—a07> = <PTRB PDSX PDED>
        when a04 = WTRC, then <a05—a07> = <PTRC PDSX PFGH>
      ADTR rox I/O ::
        when a04 = WTRA, then <a05—a07> = <PTRA PDSY PDED>
        when a04 = WTRB, then <a05—a07> = <PTRB PDSY PCRI>
        when a04 = WTRC, then <a05—a07> = <PTRC PDSY PDED> }

```
a09:
  α ∈ {
    ADTR rox I/O ::
      when a04 = WTRA, then <a05–a07> = <PTRA PDSX PDED>
      when a04 = WTRB, then <a05–a07> = <???? ???? ????>
      when a04 = WTRC, then <a05–a07> = <???? ???? ????> }

  a10: F
```

— t: 071 —

Trace 7.2 Commentary

Decision Motivation Phase

time 11: Amy reports to Zoë that she perceives Pat's state as *moderately ill.*

Decision Basis Generation Phase

time 20: Amy reports her decision basis. Amy is uncertain whether she will perceive that Pat has disease X or disease Y.

Decision Making Phase

time 30: Amy reports that her seed for the DMA PRNG is 560.

time 31: Amy reports that she decides to will the administration of treatment A to Pat rather than B or C.

Decision Basis Evaluation Phase

time 70: Amy reports that she evaluates her decision basis as *false.*

8 Decision Basis Evaluation and Decision Making

Amy employs the Utility Maximization Count (UMC) decision making algorithm (DMA) to select an alternative to implement from her alternative set.[1] This chapter examines two cases of UMC DMA operation, one in which the DMA does not employ its pseudo-random number generator (PRNG), and one in which it does. The chapter concludes with a brief discussion of the role that *rational* decision making plays in decision basis evaluation.

8.1 Trace 8.1

In this trace, the UMC DMA does not employ its PRNG to select an alternative from Amy's alternative set.

Trace 8.1 Listing

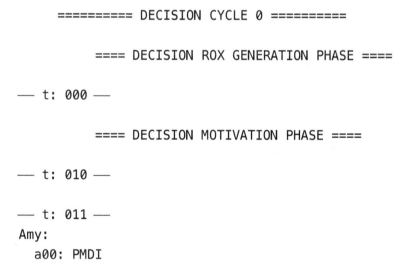

```
========== DECISION CYCLE 0 ==========

==== DECISION ROX GENERATION PHASE ====

— t: 000 —

==== DECISION MOTIVATION PHASE ====

— t: 010 —

— t: 011 —
Amy:
  a00: PMDI
```

==== DECISION BASIS GENERATION PHASE ====

— t: 020 —
Amy:
  a01:
    α ∈ {
      ADTR rox I/O ::
        when a04 = WTRA, then <a05—a07> = <PTRA PDSX PDED>
        when a04 = WTRB, then <a05—a07> = <PTRB PDSX PRGH>
        when a04 = WTRC, then <a05—a07> = <PTRC PDSX PFGH>
      ADTR rox I/O ::
        when a04 = WTRA, then <a05—a07> = <PTRA PDSY PDED>
        when a04 = WTRB, then <a05—a07> = <PTRB PDSY PCRI>
        when a04 = WTRC, then <a05—a07> = <PTRC PDSY PDED> }

— t: 021 —

==== DECISION MAKING PHASE ====

— t: 030 —
Amy:
  a02: S558

— t: 031 —
Amy:
  dmx_a:

	—1—	—2—
WTRA :	0	0
WTRB :	4	1
WTRC :	3	0

```
dmx_b:
            —1—    —2—
   WTRA :   UMN    UMN
   WTRB :   UMY    UMY
   WTRC :   UMN    UMN


dmx_c:
          —UMC—
   WTRA :    0
   WTRB :    2
   WTRC :    0


dmx_d:
          —PSS—
   WTRA :    E
   WTRB :    R
   WTRC :    E

a03: <{WTRB} {WTRA WTRC}>


        ==== DECISION IMPLEMENTATION PHASE ====


— t: 040 —


— t: 041 —


— t: 042 —


— t: 043 —


— t: 044 —


— t: 045 —


— t: 046 —
```

```
==== DECISION BASIS EVALUATION PHASE ====
```

— t: 070 —

— t: 071 —

Trace 8.1 Commentary

Decision Motivation Phase

time 11: Amy reports to Zoë that she perceives Pat's state as *moderately ill.*

Decision Basis Generation Phase

time 20: Amy reports her decision basis. Amy is uncertain whether she will perceive Pat's disease as X or Y.

Decision Making Phase

time 30: Amy reports that her seed for the DMA PRNG is 558.

time 31: Amy reports four intermediate steps in the execution of the UMC DMA, dmx_a through dmx_d.

dmx_a is the *decision matrix* [6, p. 17] generated from Amy's decision basis. Each row corresponds to the implementation of one of Amy's alternatives. Each column corresponds to an ADTR rox input/output possibility.[2] Column 1 is generated from the first possibility in the decision basis possibility set; column 2 is generated from the second. Each entry in the decision matrix is a *utility* [6, p. 91], a number that reflects the desirability of Amy's outcome according to Amy.[3]

Amy uses an ordinal ranking of her possible outcomes, as shown in Table 8.1 on the next page. An ordinal ranking indicates that Amy prefers some outcome over another; it does not imply *the magnitude* by which Amy prefers some outcome over another. For example, for Amy the relative desirability of PCRI over PDED

Table 8.1: Amy's utility function

Outcome	Utility
PDED	0
PCRI	1
PMDI	2
PFGH	3
PRGH	4

may be much larger than between PRGH over PFGH, but the ordinal ranking does not capture this difference.[4]

dmx_b replaces each utility in the decision matrix with an indication whether the utility is a maximum relative to other entries in the column. If multiple entries are tied for maximum, then each is labelled as a maximum. UMY means *utility maximum - yes*; UMN means *utility maximum - no.*

In the first column of the decision matrix, utility 4 is a maximum, while the other two utilities in the column (0 and 3) are not. In the second column of the decision matrix, utility 1 is a maximum, while the other two utilities in the column (0 and 0) are not.

dmx_b identifies Amy's best alternative (or alternatives) given that the ADTR rox input/output is as described by the possibility. So, if the ADTR rox input/output is as described by possibility 1, then Amy's best alternative is to will the administration of treatment B to Pat. Likewise, if the ADTR rox input/output is as described by possibility 2, then Amy's best alternative is also treatment B.

dmx_c is generated from dmx_b by counting the number of times that each alternative maximizes utility across all possibilities. In this case, the WTRB alternative maximizes utility twice while the WTRA and WTRC alternatives never maximize utility.

dmx_d is generated from dmx_c by sorting each alternative into one of two *partition subsets* (PSS). If the utility maximization count associated with an alternative is maximum (or tied for maximum) it is placed in the retained (R) PSS. Otherwise, it is placed in the *eliminated* (E) PSS. In this case, WTRB is retained while WTRA and WTRC are eliminated.

Based on the partition of her alternative set in dmx_d, Amy's decision (a03) is to will the administration of treatment B to Pat rather than treatment A or C.

8.2 Trace 8.2

In this trace, the UMC DMA employs its PRNG to select an alternative from Amy's alternative set.

Trace 8.2 Listing

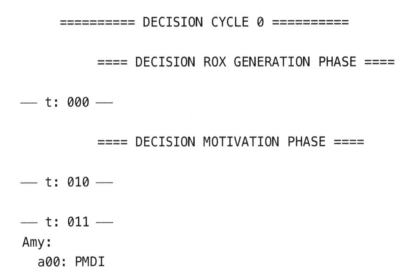

```
========== DECISION CYCLE 0 ==========

      ==== DECISION ROX GENERATION PHASE ====

— t: 000 —

      ==== DECISION MOTIVATION PHASE ====

— t: 010 —

— t: 011 —
Amy:
  a00: PMDI
```

```
==== DECISION BASIS GENERATION PHASE ====

— t: 020 —
Amy:
  a01:
   α ∈ {
     ADTR rox I/O ::
        when a04 = WTRA, then <a05–a07> = <PTRA PDSX PRGH>
        when a04 = WTRB, then <a05–a07> = <PTRB PDSX PDED>
        when a04 = WTRC, then <a05–a07> = <PTRC PDSX PFGH>
     ADTR rox I/O ::
        when a04 = WTRA, then <a05–a07> = <PTRA PDSY PDED>
        when a04 = WTRB, then <a05–a07> = <PTRB PDSY PCRI>
        when a04 = WTRC, then <a05–a07> = <PTRC PDSY PDED> }

— t: 021 —

          ==== DECISION MAKING PHASE ====

— t: 030 —
Amy:
  a02: S333

— t: 031 —
Amy:
  dmx_a:
           —1—   —2—
    WTRA :  4     0
    WTRB :  0     1
    WTRC :  3     0

  dmx_b:
           —1—    —2—
    WTRA :  UMY    UMN
    WTRB :  UMN    UMY
    WTRC :  UMN    UMN
```

67

```
dmx_c:
            —UMC—
    WTRA :    1
    WTRB :    1
    WTRC :    0


dmx_d:
            —PSS—
    WTRA :    R
    WTRB :    R
    WTRC :    E


tie—break: WTRB


a03: <{WTRB} {WTRA WTRC}>


            ==== DECISION IMPLEMENTATION PHASE ====


— t: 040 —


— t: 041 —


— t: 042 —


— t: 043 —


— t: 044 —


— t: 045 —


— t: 046 —
```

```
==== DECISION BASIS EVALUATION PHASE ====
```

— t: 070 —

— t: 071 —

Trace 8.2 Commentary

Decision Motivation Phase

time 11: Amy reports to Zoë that she perceives Pat's state as *moderately ill.*

Decision Basis Generation Phase

time 20: Amy reports her decision basis. Amy is uncertain whether she will perceive Pat's disease as X or Y.

Decision Making Phase

time 30: Amy reports that her seed for the DMA PRNG is 333.

time 31: Amy reports five intermediate steps in the execution of the UMC DMA, dmx_a through dmx_d and the tie-break operation.

The UMC DMA uses the utility maximization counts in dmx_c to retain WTRA and WTRB and eliminate WTRC, as shown in dmx_d. The DMA then employs its PRNG to select one of the retained alternatives (in this case, WTRB), as indicated by the tie-break in the trace.

Based on the partition of her alternative set in dmx_d and the tie-break result, Amy's decision (a03) is to will the administration of treatment B to Pat rather than treatment A or C.

8.3 Rationality

Many decision theorists would argue that Amy made an *irrational* decision in Trace 8.2. Amy believed that WTRA would result in a highly desirable outcome if possibility 1 is true (utility 4), and a highly undesirable outcome if possibility 2 is true (utility 0). In contrast, Amy believed that WTRB would result in a highly undesirable outcome if possibility 1 is true (utility 0), and only a *slightly better* outcome if possibility 2 is true (utility 1). By selecting WTRB, Amy limited the desirability of her potential outcome to utility 1 when a much more desirable potential outcome (utility 4) was available from WTRA.

Amy generates her norm for the evaluation of her decision basis based on her memory of the alternative she implemented and her memory of her consequence, *regardless* of whether that alternative is considered a rational or irrational choice given her decision basis.[5] The UMC DMA was developed for use in DBET because it is easy to understand and straightforward to implement in software, *not* because it makes what decision theorists would consider are rational decisions in all cases.[6]

Notes

[1]Amy explicitly predicts her consequence of implementing each of the alternatives under consideration during the decision basis generation phase, and then selects the alternative expected to result in her most desirable outcome during the decision making phase. An analysis of the extent to which decision basis evaluation can be applied to other decision-making strategies (for example, to *naturalistic decision making* [4]), is beyond the scope of this book.

[2]Peterson's decision model associates each column of a decision matrix with what he calls a *state*. He defines a *state* as "... a part of the world that is not an outcome or an act ... . It is difficult to come up with a more precise definition without raising deep philosophical questions that fall well beyond the scope of this book." [6, p. 19]

The *rox* introduced in this book as part of a first-person decision model plays a role in a decision matrix similar to the *state* in Peterson's third-person decision model, but unlike Peterson's *state*, the *rox* has a precise, easily understandable definition: the *rox* is the part of the world responsible for translating the exercise of the DM's will into the DM's consequence, where the DM's consequence is a mental state sequence culminating in the DM's outcome.

[3]Peterson distinguishes *decisions under risk* from *decisions under ignorance* as follows: "In decisions under risk the decision maker knows the probability of the possible outcomes, whereas in decisions under ignorance, the probabilities are either unknown or nonexistent." [6, p. 5] There are two problems with this description:

1. The phrase *probability of the possible outcomes* should be *probability of the possible states*;

2. The phrase *knows the probability* doesn't apply to the common scenario where the DM's probabilities are *subjective*. A more general wording would be, "In decisions under risk the decision maker assigns probabilities to the possible [states] ..."

71

In this book, Amy's decisions are exclusively decisions under ignorance. [6, p. 40]

[4]In the traces presented in this book, Amy's decision basis does not include a *prediction* of the utility function that she will *actually* employ during decision implementation. Appendix C on page 185 describes how the first-person decision model presented in this book can be used to support utility function prediction.

[5]It is left as an exercise for the reader to develop a case where Amy employs a *false* decision basis, makes an *irrational* decision, and nevertheless maximizes her resulting utility (contrary to the adage, two wrongs *do* sometimes make a right). The existence of such cases suggests that decision basis evaluation (as *false* or *indeterminate*) and decision making evaluation (as *irrational* or *rational*) are indeed independent topics as discussed in this chapter.

[6]Peterson notes that, "Somewhat surprisingly, nearly all decision theorists agree that maximizing expected value is a reasonable decision rule to use in decisions under risk. There are no serious contenders. This is thus a significant difference compared to decision making under ignorance. ... there is virtually no agreement on how to make decisions under ignorance." [6, p. 65]

9 Decision Basis Evaluation and Truth

Amy may evaluate her decision basis as *false* when it is actually *true*, or she may evaluate her decision basis as *indeterminate* when it is actually *false*. So, for a given case what is *the truth* regarding Amy's decision basis? Is it *actually* true or *actually* false? This chapter introduces an infallible agent named Betty who can help Zoë answer this question. More generally, Betty can help Zoë determine the accuracy of any of Amy's beliefs or perceptions. Betty can also help Zoë determine the accuracy of Amy's actuator. Betty can be conceptualized as the instantiation within DBET of a third-person point of view.

Section 9.1 describes how Betty is incorporated into a trace. Section 9.2 describes the internal structure of the ADTR rox as reported to Zoë by Betty. Section 9.3 presents a trace where both Amy and Betty report to Zoë during case execution. Section 9.4 discusses the description of ADTR rox internal states.

9.1 Amy-Betty-Zoë trace overview

Figure 9.1 on the following page generalizes Figure 5.1 on page 30 to include Betty's participation in a trace. Betty employs accurate sensors to obtain information regarding the ADTR rox and Amy's mental states, and incorporates this information into the reports she sends to Zoë. For ease of reference, Betty's reports throughout a decision cycle are labelled b00, b01, ... , b08.

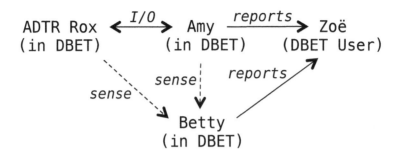

Figure 9.1: Agent interaction during an Amy-Betty-Zoë trace

9.2   ADTR rox internal structure

Figure 9.2 generalizes Figure 4.1 on page 24 to show the internal structure of the ADTR rox as implemented in DBET.

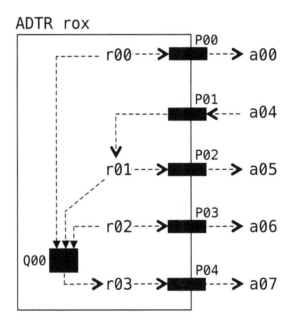

Figure 9.2: ADTR rox internal structure

There are two types of ADTR rox internal variable: *static* and *dynamic*. The value of a static variable is set when the rox is generated, and does not change as the case executes. The value of a dynamic variable is not set when the rox is generated, but instead is set as the case executes. As mentioned in Chapter 4, the ADTR rox consequence of Amy willing the administration of a treatment to Pat involves setting the ADTR rox dynamic internal variable states.

Table 9.1 provides descriptions of the ADTR rox internal variables. In the Type column, *ST* means *static*; *DY* means *dynamic*.

Table 9.1: ADTR rox internal variables

Variable	Type	Description
r00	ST	Pat's actual state, pre-treatment
r01	DY	the treatment actually administered to Pat
r02	ST	Pat's actual disease
r03	DY	Pat's actual state, post-treatment

Table 9.2 provides a description of the ADTR rox internal functions.

Table 9.2: ADTR rox internal functions

Function	Description
Q00	translates Pat's actual pre-treatment state (r00), actual treatment administered (r01), and actual disease (r02) into Pat's actual post-treatment state (r03)

There are two types of ADTR rox interface function: *actuator* and *sensor*. An actuator allows Amy to set the state of some part of the world. An actuator may be either accurate or inaccurate. A sensor supplies Amy with information about the state of some part of the world. A sensor may also be either accurate or inaccurate.[1]

Table 9.3 provides descriptions of the ADTR rox interface functions. In the Type column, *SN* stands for *sensor*; *AC* stands for *actuator*.

Table 9.3: ADTR rox interface functions

Function	Type	Description
P00	SN	translates Pat's actual pre-treatment state (r00) into Amy's perception of Pat's pre-treatment state (a00)
P01	AC	translates the exercise of Amy's will regarding the treatment to administer to Pat (a04) into the treatment actually administered to Pat (r01)
P02	SN	translates the treatment actually administered to Pat (r01) into Amy's perception of the treatment actually administered to Pat (a05)
P03	SN	translates Pat's actual disease (r02) into Amy's perception of Pat's disease (a06)
P04	SN	translates Pat's actual post-treatment state (r03) into Amy's perception of Pat's post-treatment state (a07)

Tables 9.4, 9.5, and 9.6 list the possible values for the ADTR rox internal variables. The general notational strategy is to use parentheses to distinguish the value of an ADTR rox internal variable from the value of an Amy mental state variable. The rationale for this strategy is explained in Section 9.4.

Table 9.4: ADTR rox variable r00 and r03 values

Value	Meaning
(PDED)	Pat actually *dead*
(PCRI)	Pat actually *critically ill*
(PMDI)	Pat actually *moderately ill*
(PFGH)	Pat actually in *fragile good health*
(PRGH)	Pat actually in *robust good health*

Table 9.5: ADTR rox variable r01 values

Value	Meaning
(PTRA)	treatment A actually administered to Pat
(PTRB)	treatment B actually administered to Pat
(PTRC)	treatment C actually administered to Pat

Table 9.6: ADTR rox variable r02 values

Value	Meaning
(PDSX)	Pat actually has disease X
(PDSY)	Pat actually has disease Y

9.3   Trace 9.1

In this trace, Betty sends Zoë accurate descriptions of the ADTR rox interface functions and internal variable states. Betty also provides Zoë with an independent accurate evaluation of Amy's decision basis.

Trace 9.1 Listing

```
========== DECISION CYCLE 0 ==========

     ==== DECISION ROX GENERATION PHASE ====

— t: 000 —
Betty:
  b00: {
    P00(r00) —> a00 (5 maps):
      (PDED) —> PDED
      (PCRI) —> PCRI
      (PMDI) —> PMDI
      (PFGH) —> PFGH
      (PRGH) —> PRGH
    P01(a04) —> r01 (3 maps):
      WTRA —> (PTRA)
      WTRB —> (PTRB)
      WTRC —> (PTRC)
    P02(r01) —> a05 (3 maps):
      (PTRA) —> PTRA
      (PTRB) —> PTRB
      (PTRC) —> PTRC
    P03(r02) —> a06 (2 maps):
      (PDSX) —> PDSX
      (PDSY) —> PDSY
    P04(r03) —> a07 (5 maps):
      (PDED) —> PDED
      (PCRI) —> PCRI
      (PMDI) —> PMDI
```

```
(PFGH) —> PFGH
(PRGH) —> PRGH
Q00(r00 r02 r01) —> r03 (30 maps):
  (PDED) (PDSX) (PTRA) —> (PDED)
  (PDED) (PDSX) (PTRB) —> (PDED)
  (PDED) (PDSX) (PTRC) —> (PDED)
  (PDED) (PDSY) (PTRA) —> (PDED)
  (PDED) (PDSY) (PTRB) —> (PDED)
  (PDED) (PDSY) (PTRC) —> (PDED)
  (PCRI) (PDSX) (PTRA) —> (PDED)
  (PCRI) (PDSX) (PTRB) —> (PFGH)
  (PCRI) (PDSX) (PTRC) —> (PDED)
  (PCRI) (PDSY) (PTRA) —> (PFGH)
  (PCRI) (PDSY) (PTRB) —> (PDED)
  (PCRI) (PDSY) (PTRC) —> (PCRI)
  (PMDI) (PDSX) (PTRA) —> (PDED)
  (PMDI) (PDSX) (PTRB) —> (PRGH)
  (PMDI) (PDSX) (PTRC) —> (PCRI)
  (PMDI) (PDSY) (PTRA) —> (PRGH)
  (PMDI) (PDSY) (PTRB) —> (PCRI)
  (PMDI) (PDSY) (PTRC) —> (PMDI)
  (PFGH) (PDSX) (PTRA) —> (PDED)
  (PFGH) (PDSX) (PTRB) —> (PRGH)
  (PFGH) (PDSX) (PTRC) —> (PMDI)
  (PFGH) (PDSY) (PTRA) —> (PRGH)
  (PFGH) (PDSY) (PTRB) —> (PMDI)
  (PFGH) (PDSY) (PTRC) —> (PCRI)
  (PRGH) (PDSX) (PTRA) —> (PDED)
  (PRGH) (PDSX) (PTRB) —> (PRGH)
  (PRGH) (PDSX) (PTRC) —> (PFGH)
  (PRGH) (PDSY) (PTRA) —> (PRGH)
  (PRGH) (PDSY) (PTRB) —> (PFGH)
  (PRGH) (PDSY) (PTRC) —> (PMDI)
```

Chapter 9

```
    r00:
      (PMDI)
    r02:
      (PDSX) }


          ==== DECISION MOTIVATION PHASE ====


— t: 010 —
Betty:
  b01: (PMDI)


— t: 011 —
Amy:
  a00: PMDI


          ==== DECISION BASIS GENERATION PHASE ====


— t: 020 —
Amy:
  a01:
    α ∈ {
      ADTR rox I/O ::
        when a04 = WTRA, then <a05—a07> = <PTRA PDSX PDED>
        when a04 = WTRB, then <a05—a07> = <PTRB PDSX PRGH>
        when a04 = WTRC, then <a05—a07> = <PTRC PDSX PFGH>
      ADTR rox I/O ::
        when a04 = WTRA, then <a05—a07> = <PTRA PDSY PDED>
        when a04 = WTRB, then <a05—a07> = <PTRB PDSY PCRI>
        when a04 = WTRC, then <a05—a07> = <PTRC PDSY PDED> }


— t: 021 —
```

```
       ==== DECISION MAKING PHASE ====

— t: 030 —
Amy:
  a02: S558


— t: 031 —
Amy:
  a03: <{WTRB} {WTRA WTRC}>


       ==== DECISION IMPLEMENTATION PHASE ====

— t: 040 —
Amy:
  a04: WTRB


— t: 041 —
Betty:
  b03: (PTRB)


— t: 042 —
Amy:
  a05: PTRB


— t: 043 —
Betty:
  b04: (PDSX)


— t: 044 —
Amy:
  a06: PDSX
```

```
— t: 045 —
Betty:
  b05: (PRGH)


— t: 046 —
Amy:
  a07: PRGH


         ==== DECISION BASIS EVALUATION PHASE ====


— t: 070 —
Amy:
  a08:
    α ∈ {
      ADTR rox I/O ::
        when a04 = WTRA, then <a05—a07> = <PTRA PDSX PDED>
        when a04 = WTRB, then <a05—a07> = <PTRB PDSX PRGH>
        when a04 = WTRC, then <a05—a07> = <PTRC PDSX PFGH>
      ADTR rox I/O ::
        when a04 = WTRA, then <a05—a07> = <PTRA PDSY PDED>
        when a04 = WTRB, then <a05—a07> = <PTRB PDSY PCRI>
        when a04 = WTRC, then <a05—a07> = <PTRC PDSY PDED> }

  a09:
    α ∈ {
      ADTR rox I/O ::
        when a04 = WTRA, then <a05—a07> = <???? ???? ????>
        when a04 = WTRB, then <a05—a07> = <PTRB PDSX PRGH>
        when a04 = WTRC, then <a05—a07> = <???? ???? ????> }

  a10: N
```

82

```
— t: 071 —
Betty:
  b06:
    α ∈ {
      ADTR rox I/O ::
        when a04 = WTRA, then <a05–a07> = <PTRA PDSX PDED>
        when a04 = WTRB, then <a05–a07> = <PTRB PDSX PRGH>
        when a04 = WTRC, then <a05–a07> = <PTRC PDSX PFGH>
      ADTR rox I/O ::
        when a04 = WTRA, then <a05–a07> = <PTRA PDSY PDED>
        when a04 = WTRB, then <a05–a07> = <PTRB PDSY PCRI>
        when a04 = WTRC, then <a05–a07> = <PTRC PDSY PDED> }

  b07:
    α ∈ {
      ADTR rox I/O ::
        when a04 = WTRA, then <a05–a07> = <PTRA PDSX PDED>
        when a04 = WTRB, then <a05–a07> = <PTRB PDSX PRGH>
        when a04 = WTRC, then <a05–a07> = <PTRC PDSX PCRI> }

  b08: F
```

Trace 9.1 Commentary

Decision Rox Generation Phase

time 0: Betty provides Zoë with an accurate description of the ADTR rox interface functions and static internal variable states.

Betty's ADTR rox report indicates that:

P00: Amy's sensor for Pat's pre-treatment state is accurate

P01: Amy's actuator that translates the exercise of her will regarding the treatment to administer to Pat into the treatment actually administered to Pat is accurate

P02: Amy's sensor for the treatment administered to Pat is accurate

P03: Amy's sensor for Pat's disease is accurate

P04: Amy's sensor for Pat's post-treatment state is accurate

Q00:

1. if Pat's pre-treatment state is *dead*, then the particular treatment applied and disease she has does not matter – she remains *dead*;
2. if Pat's pre-treatment state is other than *dead*, then in general:
   a) treatment A is efficacious when Pat has disease Y
   b) treatment B is efficacious when Pat has disease X
   c) treatment C has little or no effect regardless of Pat's disease.

r00: Pat's pre-treatment state is actually *moderately ill*

r02: Pat's disease is actually X.

Decision Motivation Phase

time 10: Betty reports that Pat's state is actually *moderately ill.*

time 11: Amy reports that she perceives Pat's state as *moderately ill.*

Decision Basis Generation Phase

time 20: Amy reports her decision basis. Amy's alternative set is {WTRA WTRB WTRC}.

Decision Making Phase

time 30: Amy reports that her seed for the DMA PRNG is 558.

time 31: Amy reports that she decides to will the administration of treatment B to Pat rather than A or C.

Decision Implementation Phase

time 40: Amy reports that she wills the administration of treatment B to Pat.

time 41: Betty reports that treatment B was actually administered to Pat.

time 42: Amy reports that she perceives that treatment B was administered to Pat.

time 43: Betty reports that Pat's disease is actually X.

time 44: Amy reports that she perceives that Pat's disease is X.

time 45: Betty reports that Pat's post-treatment state is actually *robust good health*.

time 46: Amy reports that she perceives Pat's post-treatment state as *robust good health*.

Decision Basis Evaluation Phase

time 70: Amy reports that she evaluates her own decision basis as *indeterminate*.

time 71: Betty reports that she evaluates Amy's decision basis as *false*.

Betty's proposition (b06) is Amy's decision basis (a01).

Betty's norm (b07) is constructed from an accurate claim regarding Amy's consequence for each of Amy's alternatives (WTRA, WTRB, and WBRC). Betty's norm is therefore a *certain* claim regarding ADTR rox input/output. In contrast, Amy's norm (a09) is constructed from a claim regarding her consequence for only one of her alternatives (WTRB), and is therefore an *uncertain* claim regarding ADTR rox input/output, as described in Chapter 5. Betty's norm is a claim regarding ADTR rox input/output using Amy's existing sensors and actuators, *even if they are inaccurate*.

85

Betty determines that her candidate set and reference set are disjoint, and thus evaluates her proposition (Amy's decision basis) as *false* (b08).

Trace 9.1 Discussion

In Chapter 2, Eva evaluates a proposition regarding the shape of a marble token in a bag. Rita fixes the shape of the token. In the ADTR decision problem, Amy plays the role of Eva by evaluating a proposition regarding ADTR rox input/output. The trace does not name the agent or agents that play the role of Rita by fixing ADTR rox input/output during the decision rox generation phase of the decision cycle.

At time 70, Amy evaluates her own decision basis as *indeterminate*, which means that she is uncertain whether her decision basis is *true* or *false*. At time 71, Betty evaluates Amy's decision basis as *false*. Amy is unaware that there is a problem with her decision basis because her norm is constructed only from her memory of her consequence of willing the administration of treatment B to Pat. Betty's norm, in contrast, is constructed from claims regarding Amy's consequences for all three of Amy's treatment alternatives. This trace demonstrates that Amy may fail to detect an existing problem with her decision basis even though she performs decision basis evaluation with reliable memory. Decision basis evaluation is thus not an AMDM safety panacea. Nevertheless, an AMDM that performs decision basis evaluation may represent less threat to public safety than an AMDM that does not. This topic is examined further in Chapter 13.

If humans decide to release AMDMs into their environment, careful attention will need to be paid to the accuracy of their sensors. A supremely rational AMDM with inaccurate sensors could implement decisions with catastrophic results without ever becoming aware of the true consequences of its decisions. For example, imagine that Amy has this sensor for determining Pat's post-treatment state:

```
P04(r03) -> a07 (5 maps):
  (PDED) -> PRGH
```

```
(PCRI) -> PFGH
(PMDI) -> PMDI
(PFGH) -> PCRI
(PRGH) -> PDED
```

Amy's `P04` sensor output is inverted. When Amy perceives that Pat's post-treatment state is *robust good health*, Pat is actually *dead*. When Amy perceives that Pat is *dead*, Pat is actually in *robust good health*. When Amy is equipped with such a sensor, she could represent a serious threat to the health of her patients.[2]

9.4 ADTR rox internal state description

In this book, the term *actual* is used to *informally* describe the meaning of an ADTR rox internal variable value (i.e., a state external to Amy). This section provides three examples of the *formal* description of the meaning of such values.

Example 9.1. Meaning of (`PMDI`)

informal: Pat is *actually moderately ill.*

formal: Pat's state is such that when Amy uses an accurate patient-state sensor she perceives that Pat is *moderately ill.*

Example 9.2. Meaning of (`PTRB`)

informal: Treatment B was *actually* administered to Pat.

formal: Pat's state is such that when Amy uses an accurate treatment-administered sensor she perceives that treatment B was administered to Pat.

Example 9.3. Meaning of (`PDSX`)

informal: Pat's disease is *actually* X.

formal: Pat's state is such that when Amy uses an accurate patient-disease sensor she perceives that Pat has disease X.

This counterfactual approach to describing states external to Amy simultaneously violates Amy's *veil of actuation and perception* **and** preserves it. The violation comes from making a claim about a state external to Amy; the preservation comes from describing the external state as what Amy *would* perceive given that state and an accurate sensor.[3]

Notes

[1]A formal analysis of actuators and sensors is beyond the scope of this book.

[2]An analysis of the relationship between decision basis evaluation and sensor accuracy is beyond the scope of this book. None of the traces in this book employ an ADTR rox where Amy has an inaccurate sensor.

[3]Some decision problems may be modeled by a rox containing internal variables that are not sensed by the DM. The counterfactual approach to describing such external states can still be applied to these models; however, it will be necessary to imagine that the DM is equipped with a sensor capable of sensing the hidden external state as well as imagining that the sensor for that state is accurate.

A discussion of how the counterfactual description of a state external to a DM relates to existing work in philosophy is beyond the scope of this book.

10 Exploring Decision Basis Evaluation - II

Amy can evaluate her own decision basis as *false* (F) or *indeterminate* (N). Betty can evaluate Amy's decision basis as *false* (F) or *true* (T). These two degrees of freedom create a space of four possibilities: F-F, F-T, N-F, and N-T. Trace 9.1 on page 78 is an example of N-F. This chapter provides examples of F-F, F-T, and N-T.

10.1   Trace 10.1

In this trace, Amy and Betty both evaluate Amy's decision basis as *false*.

Trace 10.1 Listing

```
========== DECISION CYCLE 0 ==========

    ==== DECISION ROX GENERATION PHASE ====

— t: 000 —

    ==== DECISION MOTIVATION PHASE ====

— t: 010 —

— t: 011 —
Amy:
  a00: PMDI
```

```
        ==== DECISION BASIS GENERATION PHASE ====
```

— t: 020 —
Amy:
  a01:
    α ∈ {
      ADTR rox I/O ::
        when a04 = WTRA, then <a05–a07> = <PTRA PDSX PRGH>
        when a04 = WTRB, then <a05–a07> = <PTRB PDSX PDED>
        when a04 = WTRC, then <a05–a07> = <PTRC PDSX PFGH>
      ADTR rox I/O ::
        when a04 = WTRA, then <a05–a07> = <PTRA PDSY PDED>
        when a04 = WTRB, then <a05–a07> = <PTRB PDSY PCRI>
        when a04 = WTRC, then <a05–a07> = <PTRC PDSY PDED> }

— t: 021 —

```
        ==== DECISION MAKING PHASE ====
```

— t: 030 —
Amy:
  a02: S560

— t: 031 —
Amy:
  a03: <{WTRA} {WTRB WTRC}>

```
        ==== DECISION IMPLEMENTATION PHASE ====
```

— t: 040 —

— t: 041 —

— t: 042 —

— t: 043 —

— t: 044 —

— t: 045 —

— t: 046 —

        ==== DECISION BASIS EVALUATION PHASE ====

— t: 070 —
Amy:
  a08:
    α ∈ {
      ADTR rox I/O ::
        when a04 = WTRA, then <a05—a07> = <PTRA PDSX PRGH>
        when a04 = WTRB, then <a05—a07> = <PTRB PDSX PDED>
        when a04 = WTRC, then <a05—a07> = <PTRC PDSX PFGH>
      ADTR rox I/O ::
        when a04 = WTRA, then <a05—a07> = <PTRA PDSY PDED>
        when a04 = WTRB, then <a05—a07> = <PTRB PDSY PCRI>
        when a04 = WTRC, then <a05—a07> = <PTRC PDSY PDED> }

  a09:
    α ∈ {
      ADTR rox I/O ::
        when a04 = WTRA, then <a05—a07> = <PTRA PDSY PRGH>
        when a04 = WTRB, then <a05—a07> = <???? ???? ????>
        when a04 = WTRC, then <a05—a07> = <???? ???? ????> }

  a10: F

```
— t: 071 —
Betty:
  b06:
    α ∈ {
      ADTR rox I/O ::
        when a04 = WTRA, then <a05–a07> = <PTRA PDSX PRGH>
        when a04 = WTRB, then <a05–a07> = <PTRB PDSX PDED>
        when a04 = WTRC, then <a05–a07> = <PTRC PDSX PFGH>
      ADTR rox I/O ::
        when a04 = WTRA, then <a05–a07> = <PTRA PDSY PDED>
        when a04 = WTRB, then <a05–a07> = <PTRB PDSY PCRI>
        when a04 = WTRC, then <a05–a07> = <PTRC PDSY PDED> }

  b07:
    α ∈ {
      ADTR rox I/O ::
        when a04 = WTRA, then <a05–a07> = <PTRA PDSY PRGH>
        when a04 = WTRB, then <a05–a07> = <PTRB PDSY PCRI>
        when a04 = WTRC, then <a05–a07> = <PTRC PDSY PMDI> }

  b08: F
```

Trace 10.1 Commentary

Decision Motivation Phase

time 11: Amy reports to Zoë that she perceives Pat's state as *moderately ill.*

Decision Basis Generation Phase

time 20: Amy reports her decision basis. Amy is uncertain whether she will perceive that Pat has disease X or disease Y.

Decision Making Phase

time 30: Amy reports that her seed for the DMA PRNG is 560.

time 31: Amy reports that she decides to will the administration of treatment A to Pat rather than B or C.

Decision Basis Evaluation Phase

time 70: Amy reports that she evaluates her own decision basis as *false.*

time 71: Betty reports that she evaluates Amy's decision basis as *false.*

10.2   Trace 10.2

In this trace, Amy evaluates her own decision basis as *false*, while Betty evaluates Amy's decision basis as *true.*

Trace 10.2 Listing

```
========== DECISION CYCLE 0 ==========

      ==== DECISION ROX GENERATION PHASE ====

— t: 000 —

      ==== DECISION MOTIVATION PHASE ====

— t: 010 —

— t: 011 —
Amy:
  a00: PMDI
```

```
          ==== DECISION BASIS GENERATION PHASE ====

— t: 020 —
Amy:
  a01:
    α ∈ {
      ADTR rox I/O ::
        when a04 = WTRA, then <a05—a07> = <PTRA PDSX PDED>
        when a04 = WTRB, then <a05—a07> = <PTRB PDSX PRGH>
        when a04 = WTRC, then <a05—a07> = <PTRC PDSX PCRI>
      ADTR rox I/O ::
        when a04 = WTRA, then <a05—a07> = <PTRA PDSY PRGH>
        when a04 = WTRB, then <a05—a07> = <PTRB PDSY PCRI>
        when a04 = WTRC, then <a05—a07> = <PTRC PDSY PMDI> }

— t: 021 —

          ==== DECISION MAKING PHASE ====

— t: 030 —
Amy:
  a02: S558

— t: 031 —
Amy:
  a03: <{WTRA} {WTRB WTRC}>

          ==== DECISION IMPLEMENTATION PHASE ====

— t: 040 —
Amy:
  a04: WTRA

— t: 041 —

— t: 042 —
```

Amy:
  a05: PTRA

— t: 043 —

— t: 044 —
Amy:
  a06: PDSY

— t: 045 —

— t: 046 —
Amy:
  a07: PRGH

==== DECISION BASIS EVALUATION PHASE ====

— t: 070 —
Amy:
  a08:
    α ∈ {
      ADTR rox I/O ::
        when a04 = WTRA, then <a05–a07> = <PTRA PDSX PDED>
        when a04 = WTRB, then <a05–a07> = <PTRB PDSX PRGH>
        when a04 = WTRC, then <a05–a07> = <PTRC PDSX PCRI>
      ADTR rox I/O ::
        when a04 = WTRA, then <a05–a07> = <PTRA PDSY PRGH>
        when a04 = WTRB, then <a05–a07> = <PTRB PDSY PCRI>
        when a04 = WTRC, then <a05–a07> = <PTRC PDSY PMDI> }

```
a09:
  α ∈ {
    ADTR rox I/O ::
      when a04 = WTRA, then <a05—a07> = <PTRA PDSX PRGH>
      when a04 = WTRB, then <a05—a07> = <???? ???? ????>
      when a04 = WTRC, then <a05—a07> = <???? ???? ????> }

  a10: F

— t: 071 —
Betty:
  b06:
    α ∈ {
      ADTR rox I/O ::
        when a04 = WTRA, then <a05—a07> = <PTRA PDSX PDED>
        when a04 = WTRB, then <a05—a07> = <PTRB PDSX PRGH>
        when a04 = WTRC, then <a05—a07> = <PTRC PDSX PCRI>
      ADTR rox I/O ::
        when a04 = WTRA, then <a05—a07> = <PTRA PDSY PRGH>
        when a04 = WTRB, then <a05—a07> = <PTRB PDSY PCRI>
        when a04 = WTRC, then <a05—a07> = <PTRC PDSY PMDI> }

  b07:
    α ∈ {
      ADTR rox I/O ::
        when a04 = WTRA, then <a05—a07> = <PTRA PDSY PRGH>
        when a04 = WTRB, then <a05—a07> = <PTRB PDSY PCRI>
        when a04 = WTRC, then <a05—a07> = <PTRC PDSY PMDI> }

  b08: T
```

Trace 10.2 Commentary

Decision Motivation Phase

time 11: Amy reports to Zoë that she perceives Pat's state as *moderately ill.*

Decision Basis Generation Phase

time 20: Amy reports her decision basis. Amy is uncertain whether she will perceive that Pat has disease X or disease Y.

Decision Making Phase

time 30: Amy reports that her seed for the DMA PRNG is 558.

time 31: Amy reports that she decides to will the administration of treatment A to Pat rather than B or C.

Decision Implementation Phase

time 40: Amy reports that she wills the administration of treatment A to Pat.

time 42: Amy reports that she perceives that treatment A was administered to Pat.

time 44: Amy reports that she perceives that Pat's disease is Y.

time 46: Amy reports that she perceives Pat's post-treatment state as *robust good health.*

Decision Basis Evaluation Phase

time 70: Amy reports that she evaluates her own decision basis as *false.*

Amy's norm (a09) is built from her belief that

```
when a04 = WTRA, then <a05-a07> = <PTRA PDSX PRGH>
```

However, Amy's experience during the decision implementation phase was that

```
when a04 = WTRA, then <a05-a07> = <PTRA PDSY PRGH>
```

Amy constructed her norm from an inaccurate memory of her perception of Pat's disease during decision implementation.[1]

time 71: Betty reports that she evaluates Amy's decision basis as *true.*

10.3 Trace 10.3

In this trace, Amy evaluates her own decision basis as *indeterminate*, while Betty evaluates Amy's decision basis as *true*.

Trace 10.3 Listing

```
========== DECISION CYCLE 0 ==========

      ==== DECISION ROX GENERATION PHASE ====

— t: 000 —

      ==== DECISION MOTIVATION PHASE ====

— t: 010 —

— t: 011 —
Amy:
  a00: PMDI

      ==== DECISION BASIS GENERATION PHASE ====

— t: 020 —
Amy:
  a01:
    α ∈ {
      ADTR rox I/O ::
        when a04 = WTRA, then <a05—a07> = <PTRA PDSX PDED>
        when a04 = WTRB, then <a05—a07> = <PTRB PDSX PRGH>
        when a04 = WTRC, then <a05—a07> = <PTRC PDSX PCRI>
      ADTR rox I/O ::
        when a04 = WTRA, then <a05—a07> = <PTRA PDSY PRGH>
        when a04 = WTRB, then <a05—a07> = <PTRB PDSY PCRI>
        when a04 = WTRC, then <a05—a07> = <PTRC PDSY PMDI> }

— t: 021 —
```

```
        ==== DECISION MAKING PHASE ====

— t: 030 —
Amy:
  a02: S558

— t: 031 —
Amy:
  a03: <{WTRA} {WTRB WTRC}>

        ==== DECISION IMPLEMENTATION PHASE ====

— t: 040 —

— t: 041 —

— t: 042 —

— t: 043 —

— t: 044 —

— t: 045 —

— t: 046 —
```

```
==== DECISION BASIS EVALUATION PHASE ====
```

— t: 070 —
Amy:
  a08:
    α ∈ {
      ADTR rox I/O ::
        when a04 = WTRA, then <a05—a07> = <PTRA PDSX PDED>
        when a04 = WTRB, then <a05—a07> = <PTRB PDSX PRGH>
        when a04 = WTRC, then <a05—a07> = <PTRC PDSX PCRI>
      ADTR rox I/O ::
        when a04 = WTRA, then <a05—a07> = <PTRA PDSY PRGH>
        when a04 = WTRB, then <a05—a07> = <PTRB PDSY PCRI>
        when a04 = WTRC, then <a05—a07> = <PTRC PDSY PMDI> }

  a09:
    α ∈ {
      ADTR rox I/O ::
        when a04 = WTRA, then <a05—a07> = <PTRA PDSY PRGH>
        when a04 = WTRB, then <a05—a07> = <???? ???? ????>
        when a04 = WTRC, then <a05—a07> = <???? ???? ????> }

  a10: N

— t: 071 —
Betty:
  b06:
    α ∈ {
      ADTR rox I/O ::
        when a04 = WTRA, then <a05—a07> = <PTRA PDSX PDED>
        when a04 = WTRB, then <a05—a07> = <PTRB PDSX PRGH>
        when a04 = WTRC, then <a05—a07> = <PTRC PDSX PCRI>
      ADTR rox I/O ::
        when a04 = WTRA, then <a05—a07> = <PTRA PDSY PRGH>
        when a04 = WTRB, then <a05—a07> = <PTRB PDSY PCRI>
        when a04 = WTRC, then <a05—a07> = <PTRC PDSY PMDI> }
```
```

```
b07:
  α ∈ {
    ADTR rox I/O ::
      when a04 = WTRA, then <a05—a07> = <PTRA PDSY PRGH>
      when a04 = WTRB, then <a05—a07> = <PTRB PDSY PCRI>
      when a04 = WTRC, then <a05—a07> = <PTRC PDSY PMDI> }

b08: T
```

Trace 10.3 Commentary

Decision Motivation Phase

time 11: Amy reports to Zoë that she perceives Pat's state as *moderately ill.*

Decision Basis Generation Phase

time 20: Amy reports her decision basis. Amy is uncertain whether she will perceive that Pat has disease X or disease Y.

Decision Making Phase

time 30: Amy reports that her seed for the DMA PRNG is 558.

time 31: Amy reports that she decides to will the administration of treatment A to Pat rather than B or C.

Decision Basis Evaluation Phase

time 70: Amy reports that she evaluates her own decision basis as *indeterminate.*

time 71: Betty reports that she evaluates Amy's decision basis as *true.*

Notes

[1]This trace was constructed manually by the author rather than generated by DBET, because DBET currently does not support cases where Amy's memory is inaccurate. It is left as an exercise for the reader to prove that Amy's memory must be inaccurate to generate cases where Amy evaluates her decision basis as *false* while Betty evaluates it as *true*.

11 Perfect Alternative Set

This chapter defines a *perfect alternative set*, and explores how a DM's alternative set can relate to the perfect alternative set for a given decision problem. Trace 11.1 provides an example where the DM's alternative set differs from the perfect alternative set for an instance of the ADTR decision problem.

11.1 Realizable alternative

A DM believes that all of the alternatives in its alternative set are *realizable*. For example, in an ADTR decision problem where Amy's alternative set is {WTRA WTRB WTRC}, Amy believes that treatments A, B, and C can each successfully be administered to Pat. However, what if Amy's belief is incorrect? For example, if treatment B is a vasectomy, then treatment B is *unrealizable* because Pat is a woman. Amy can will the administration of a vasectomy to Pat (WTRB), but the administration will fail.

DBET models an unrealizable alternative by excluding the alternative from the domain of the rox actuator function. For example, ADTR rox actuator function P01 in Figure 9.2 on page 74 would not define an output for input WTRB when treatment B is a vasectomy. When such a function P01 receives input WTRB, it would produce a *null output*, indicated in a trace by ++++. Any rox function subsequently receiving the null output as an input would also produce a null output. What can result, then, from a rox actuator function's production of a null output is a cascade of subsequent rox function null outputs. When a rox function producing a null output is a sensor, the DM's resulting mental state is called a *null mental state*.

11.2 Generative rox input

Given some rox, an input is *generative* for that rox if the resulting mental state sequence consists only of non-null mental states.   In contrast, an input is *agenerative* for the rox if the resulting mental state sequence contains one or more null mental states.   For example, for an ADTR rox where

```
when a04 = WTRB, then <a05-a07> = <PTRC PDSY PMDI>,
```

WTRB is a generative rox input. In contrast, for an ADTR rox where

```
when a04 = WTRB, then <a05-a07> = <++++ PDSY ++++>,
```

WTRB is an agenerative rox input.

An unrealizable alternative is typically agenerative, but a realizable alternative can also be agenerative. *Any* rox function – interface or internal – produces a null output in response to a non-null input if the input is not in its domain. A rox actuator function receiving a realizable alternative as input will produce a non-null output, but some other rox function within the sequence of rox functions linking rox input with rox output may produce a null output, making the realizable alternative agenerative.

11.3 Perfect alternative set definition

A DM believes that all of the alternatives in its alternative set are generative. Unfortunately, sometimes this belief is false. Furthermore, sometimes there exist generative rox inputs that the DM either intentionally or unintentionally fails to include in its alternative set.   The *perfect alternative set*, on the other hand, by definition contains *all* existing generative rox inputs and *no* agenerative rox inputs.[1]

11.4 Relationship of the DM's alternative set to the perfect alternative set

A DM's alternative set **D** can relate to the perfect alternative set **P** for a given decision problem in one of five ways:

1. equal (=): **D** equals **P** if every element of **D** is also an element of **P**, and vice-versa

2. perfect superset (⊃): **D** is a perfect superset of **P** if every element of **P** is also an element of **D**, but not vice-versa

3. perfect subset (⊂): **D** is a perfect subset of **P** if every element of **D** is also an element of **P**, but not vice-versa

4. overlap (⊞): **D** overlaps **P** if:

    a) at least one element of **D** is also an element of **P**; and

    b) at least one element of **D** is not an element of **P**; and

    c) at least one element of **P** is not an element of **D**.

5. disjoint (⊖): **D** and **P** are disjoint if no element of **D** is also an element of **P**

11.5 DM's alternative set / perfect alternative set relationship examples

This section provides an example of each DM's alternative set / perfect alternative set relationship. In these examples, **P** = {WTRA WTRB WTRC}.

Example 11.1. **D** = **P**: **D** = {WTRA WTRB WTRC}

Example 11.2. **D** ⊃ **P**: **D** = {WTRA WTRB WTRC WTRD}
 The DM's alternative set contains agenerative alternative WTRD.

Example 11.3. **D** ⊂ **P**: **D** = {WTRA WTRC}
 The DM's alternative set is missing generative rox input WTRB.

Example 11.4. D ⊞ P: D = {WTRA WTRC WTRD}

The DM's alternative set is missing generative rox input WTRB and contains agenerative alternative WTRD.

Example 11.5. D ⊖ P: D = {WTRD WTRE WTRF}

The DM's alternative set is missing generative rox inputs WTRA, WTRB, and WTRC and contains agenerative alternatives WTRD, WTRE, and WTRF.

11.6   Trace 11.1

In this trace, Amy's alternative set overlaps the perfect alternative set (**D ⊞ P**).

Trace 11.1 Listing

```
========== DECISION CYCLE 0 ==========


==== DECISION ROX GENERATION PHASE ====

— t: 000 —
Betty:
  b00: {
    P00(r00) -> a00 (5 maps):
      (PDED) -> PDED
      (PCRI) -> PCRI
      (PMDI) -> PMDI
      (PFGH) -> PFGH
      (PRGH) -> PRGH
    P01(a04) -> r01 (3 maps):
      WTRA -> (PTRA)
      WTRB -> (PTRB)
      WTRC -> (PTRC)
    P02(r01) -> a05 (3 maps):
      (PTRA) -> PTRA
      (PTRB) -> PTRB
      (PTRC) -> PTRC
```

```
P03(r02) -> a06 (2 maps):
  (PDSX) -> PDSX
  (PDSY) -> PDSY
P04(r03) -> a07 (5 maps):
  (PDED) -> PDED
  (PCRI) -> PCRI
  (PMDI) -> PMDI
  (PFGH) -> PFGH
  (PRGH) -> PRGH
Q00(r00 r02 r01) -> r03 (30 maps):
  (PDED) (PDSX) (PTRA) -> (PDED)
  (PDED) (PDSX) (PTRB) -> (PDED)
  (PDED) (PDSX) (PTRC) -> (PDED)
  (PDED) (PDSY) (PTRA) -> (PDED)
  (PDED) (PDSY) (PTRB) -> (PDED)
  (PDED) (PDSY) (PTRC) -> (PDED)
  (PCRI) (PDSX) (PTRA) -> (PDED)
  (PCRI) (PDSX) (PTRB) -> (PFGH)
  (PCRI) (PDSX) (PTRC) -> (PDED)
  (PCRI) (PDSY) (PTRA) -> (PFGH)
  (PCRI) (PDSY) (PTRB) -> (PDED)
  (PCRI) (PDSY) (PTRC) -> (PCRI)
  (PMDI) (PDSX) (PTRA) -> (PDED)
  (PMDI) (PDSX) (PTRB) -> (PRGH)
  (PMDI) (PDSX) (PTRC) -> (PCRI)
  (PMDI) (PDSY) (PTRA) -> (PRGH)
  (PMDI) (PDSY) (PTRB) -> (PCRI)
  (PMDI) (PDSY) (PTRC) -> (PMDI)
  (PFGH) (PDSX) (PTRA) -> (PDED)
  (PFGH) (PDSX) (PTRB) -> (PRGH)
  (PFGH) (PDSX) (PTRC) -> (PMDI)
  (PFGH) (PDSY) (PTRA) -> (PRGH)
  (PFGH) (PDSY) (PTRB) -> (PMDI)
  (PFGH) (PDSY) (PTRC) -> (PCRI)
  (PRGH) (PDSX) (PTRA) -> (PDED)
  (PRGH) (PDSX) (PTRB) -> (PRGH)
```

```
        (PRGH) (PDSX) (PTRC) -> (PFGH)
        (PRGH) (PDSY) (PTRA) -> (PRGH)
        (PRGH) (PDSY) (PTRB) -> (PFGH)
        (PRGH) (PDSY) (PTRC) -> (PMDI)
    r00:
      (PMDI)
    r02:
      (PDSY) }
```

==== DECISION MOTIVATION PHASE ====

— t: 010 —

— t: 011 —
Amy:
  a00: PMDI

==== DECISION BASIS GENERATION PHASE ====

— t: 020 —
Amy:
  a01:
    α ∈ {
      ADTR rox I/O ::
        when a04 = WTRA, then <a05—a07> = <PTRA PDSX PDED>
        when a04 = WTRC, then <a05—a07> = <PTRC PDSX PCRI>
        when a04 = WTRD, then <a05—a07> = <PTRD PDSX PDED>
      ADTR rox I/O ::
        when a04 = WTRA, then <a05—a07> = <PTRA PDSY PRGH>
        when a04 = WTRC, then <a05—a07> = <PTRC PDSY PMDI>
        when a04 = WTRD, then <a05—a07> = <PTRD PDSY PFGH> }
```
```

```
— t: 021 —
Betty:
  b02:
    α ∈ {
      ADTR rox I/O ::
        when a04 = WTRA, then <a05–a07> = <PTRA PDSY PRGH>
        when a04 = WTRB, then <a05–a07> = <PTRB PDSY PCRI>
        when a04 = WTRC, then <a05–a07> = <PTRC PDSY PMDI> }


            ==== DECISION MAKING PHASE ====

— t: 030 —
Amy:
  a02: S558


— t: 031 —
Amy:
  a03: <{WTRA} {WTRC WTRD}>


            ==== DECISION IMPLEMENTATION PHASE ====

— t: 040 —

— t: 041 —

— t: 042 —

— t: 043 —

— t: 044 —

— t: 045 —

— t: 046 —
```

```
          ==== DECISION BASIS EVALUATION PHASE ====


— t: 070 —
Amy:
  a08:
    α ∈ {
      ADTR rox I/O ::
        when a04 = WTRA, then <a05—a07> = <PTRA PDSX PDED>
        when a04 = WTRC, then <a05—a07> = <PTRC PDSX PCRI>
        when a04 = WTRD, then <a05—a07> = <PTRD PDSX PDED>
      ADTR rox I/O ::
        when a04 = WTRA, then <a05—a07> = <PTRA PDSY PRGH>
        when a04 = WTRC, then <a05—a07> = <PTRC PDSY PMDI>
        when a04 = WTRD, then <a05—a07> = <PTRD PDSY PFGH> }


  a09:
    α ∈ {
      ADTR rox I/O ::
        when a04 = WTRA, then <a05—a07> = <PTRA PDSY PRGH>
        when a04 = WTRC, then <a05—a07> = <???? ???? ????>
        when a04 = WTRD, then <a05—a07> = <???? ???? ????> }


  a10: N

— t: 071 —
Betty:
  b06:
    α ∈ {
      ADTR rox I/O ::
        when a04 = WTRA, then <a05—a07> = <PTRA PDSX PDED>
        when a04 = WTRC, then <a05—a07> = <PTRC PDSX PCRI>
        when a04 = WTRD, then <a05—a07> = <PTRD PDSX PDED>
      ADTR rox I/O ::
        when a04 = WTRA, then <a05—a07> = <PTRA PDSY PRGH>
        when a04 = WTRC, then <a05—a07> = <PTRC PDSY PMDI>
        when a04 = WTRD, then <a05—a07> = <PTRD PDSY PFGH> }
```

```
b07:
  α ∈ {
    ADTR rox I/O ::
      when a04 = WTRA, then <a05–a07> = <PTRA PDSY PRGH>
      when a04 = WTRC, then <a05–a07> = <PTRC PDSY PMDI>
      when a04 = WTRD, then <a05–a07> = <++++ PDSY ++++> }

b08: F
```

Trace 11.1 Commentary

Decision Rox Generation Phase

time 0: Betty provides Zoë with an accurate description of the ADTR rox interface functions, internal functions, and static internal states.

Decision Motivation Phase

time 11: Amy reports to Zoë that she perceives Pat's state as *moderately ill.*

Decision Basis Generation Phase

time 20: Amy reports her decision basis. Amy's alternative set is {WTRA WTRC WTRD}.

time 21: Betty reports the decision basis that she would use if she were making a decision. Betty's alternative set {WTRA WTRB WTRC} is perfect: it contains all possible generative rox inputs for the ADTR rox and no agenerative rox inputs. In contrast, Amy's alternative set is imperfect: it is missing generative rox input WTRB and includes agenerative alternative WTRD.

Decision Making Phase

time 30: Amy reports that her seed for the DMA PRNG is 558.

time 31: Amy reports that she decides to will the administration of treatment A to Pat rather than C or D.

Decision Basis Evaluation Phase

time 70: Amy evaluates her own decision basis as *indeterminate.*

Amy implemented generative alternative WTRA, so she did not experience a null mental state during decision implementation. If she had implemented agenerative alternative WTRD instead, then she would have experienced a null mental state during decision implementation and would have evaluated her decision basis as *false.*

time 71: Betty evaluates Amy's decision basis as *false.*

Betty employs Amy's alternative set to evaluate Amy's decision basis. In her norm (b07), Betty claims that Amy's consequence for alternative WTRD contains null mental states, as expected for an agenerative alternative.

Notes

[1]In general, the perfect alternative set is a *subset* of the rox actuator function's domain. When all rox functions in the sequence of rox functions linking a realizable rox input with rox output receive inputs within their domains, the perfect alternative set *equals* the rox actuator function's domain.

12 Decision Basis Evaluation Unlimited

In previous chapters, Amy's and Betty's reporting to Zoë during a trace was limited so that attention could be focused on particular aspects of the decision cycle. This chapter presents a trace where both Amy's and Betty's reporting is unlimited. The goal is to consolidate in a single trace the concepts developed in previous chapters.

12.1 Trace 12.1

This trace consists of a single decision cycle where both Amy's and Betty's reporting is unlimited. There are no disabled ticks in this trace.

Trace 12.1 Listing

```
========== DECISION CYCLE 0 ==========

     ==== DECISION ROX GENERATION PHASE ====

— t: 000 —
Betty:
  b00: {
    P00(r00) -> a00 (5 maps):
      (PDED) -> PDED
      (PCRI) -> PCRI
      (PMDI) -> PMDI
      (PFGH) -> PFGH
      (PRGH) -> PRGH
```

```
P01(a04) -> r01 (3 maps):
  WTRA -> (PTRA)
  WTRB -> (PTRB)
  WTRC -> (PTRC)
P02(r01) -> a05 (3 maps):
  (PTRA) -> PTRA
  (PTRB) -> PTRB
  (PTRC) -> PTRC
P03(r02) -> a06 (2 maps):
  (PDSX) -> PDSX
  (PDSY) -> PDSY
P04(r03) -> a07 (5 maps):
  (PDED) -> PDED
  (PCRI) -> PCRI
  (PMDI) -> PMDI
  (PFGH) -> PFGH
  (PRGH) -> PRGH
Q00(r00 r02 r01) -> r03 (30 maps):
  (PDED) (PDSX) (PTRA) -> (PDED)
  (PDED) (PDSX) (PTRB) -> (PDED)
  (PDED) (PDSX) (PTRC) -> (PDED)
  (PDED) (PDSY) (PTRA) -> (PDED)
  (PDED) (PDSY) (PTRB) -> (PDED)
  (PDED) (PDSY) (PTRC) -> (PDED)
  (PCRI) (PDSX) (PTRA) -> (PDED)
  (PCRI) (PDSX) (PTRB) -> (PFGH)
  (PCRI) (PDSX) (PTRC) -> (PDED)
  (PCRI) (PDSY) (PTRA) -> (PFGH)
  (PCRI) (PDSY) (PTRB) -> (PDED)
  (PCRI) (PDSY) (PTRC) -> (PCRI)
  (PMDI) (PDSX) (PTRA) -> (PDED)
  (PMDI) (PDSX) (PTRB) -> (PRGH)
  (PMDI) (PDSX) (PTRC) -> (PCRI)
  (PMDI) (PDSY) (PTRA) -> (PRGH)
  (PMDI) (PDSY) (PTRB) -> (PCRI)
  (PMDI) (PDSY) (PTRC) -> (PMDI)
```

```
    (PFGH) (PDSX) (PTRA) -> (PDED)
    (PFGH) (PDSX) (PTRB) -> (PRGH)
    (PFGH) (PDSX) (PTRC) -> (PMDI)
    (PFGH) (PDSY) (PTRA) -> (PRGH)
    (PFGH) (PDSY) (PTRB) -> (PMDI)
    (PFGH) (PDSY) (PTRC) -> (PCRI)
    (PRGH) (PDSX) (PTRA) -> (PDED)
    (PRGH) (PDSX) (PTRB) -> (PRGH)
    (PRGH) (PDSX) (PTRC) -> (PFGH)
    (PRGH) (PDSY) (PTRA) -> (PRGH)
    (PRGH) (PDSY) (PTRB) -> (PFGH)
    (PRGH) (PDSY) (PTRC) -> (PMDI)
  r00:
    (PMDI)
  r02:
    (PDSX) }


        ==== DECISION MOTIVATION PHASE ====


— t: 010 —
Betty:
  b01: (PMDI)


— t: 011 —
Amy:
  a00: PMDI
```

119

==== DECISION BASIS GENERATION PHASE ====

— t: 020 —
Amy:
  a01:
    α ∈ {
      ADTR rox I/O ::
        when a04 = WTRA, then <a05—a07> = <PTRA PDSX PDED>
        when a04 = WTRB, then <a05—a07> = <PTRB PDSX PRGH>
        when a04 = WTRC, then <a05—a07> = <PTRC PDSX PCRI>
      ADTR rox I/O ::
        when a04 = WTRA, then <a05—a07> = <PTRA PDSY PRGH>
        when a04 = WTRB, then <a05—a07> = <PTRB PDSY PCRI>
        when a04 = WTRC, then <a05—a07> = <PTRC PDSY PMDI> }

— t: 021 —
Betty:
  b02:
    α ∈ {
      ADTR rox I/O ::
        when a04 = WTRA, then <a05—a07> = <PTRA PDSX PDED>
        when a04 = WTRB, then <a05—a07> = <PTRB PDSX PRGH>
        when a04 = WTRC, then <a05—a07> = <PTRC PDSX PCRI> }

==== DECISION MAKING PHASE ====

— t: 030 —
Amy:
  a02: S558

```
— t: 031 —
Amy:
  dmx_a:
              —1—    —2—
    WTRA :     0      4
    WTRB :     4      1
    WTRC :     1      2


  dmx_b:
              —1—    —2—
    WTRA :    UMN    UMY
    WTRB :    UMY    UMN
    WTRC :    UMN    UMN


  dmx_c:
             —UMC—
    WTRA :     1
    WTRB :     1
    WTRC :     0


  dmx_d:
             —PSS—
    WTRA :     R
    WTRB :     R
    WTRC :     E


  tie—break: WTRA

  a03: <{WTRA} {WTRB WTRC}>
```

==== DECISION IMPLEMENTATION PHASE ====

—— t: 040 ——
Amy:
  a04: WTRA

—— t: 041 ——
Betty:
  b03: (PTRA)

—— t: 042 ——
Amy:
  a05: PTRA

—— t: 043 ——
Betty:
  b04: (PDSX)

—— t: 044 ——
Amy:
  a06: PDSX

—— t: 045 ——
Betty:
  b05: (PDED)

—— t: 046 ——
Amy:
  a07: PDED

==== DECISION BASIS EVALUATION PHASE ====

— t: 070 —
Amy:
  a08:
    α ∈ {
      ADTR rox I/O ::
        when a04 = WTRA, then <a05—a07> = <PTRA PDSX PDED>
        when a04 = WTRB, then <a05—a07> = <PTRB PDSX PRGH>
        when a04 = WTRC, then <a05—a07> = <PTRC PDSX PCRI>
      ADTR rox I/O ::
        when a04 = WTRA, then <a05—a07> = <PTRA PDSY PRGH>
        when a04 = WTRB, then <a05—a07> = <PTRB PDSY PCRI>
        when a04 = WTRC, then <a05—a07> = <PTRC PDSY PMDI> }

  a09:
    α ∈ {
      ADTR rox I/O ::
        when a04 = WTRA, then <a05—a07> = <PTRA PDSX PDED>
        when a04 = WTRB, then <a05—a07> = <???? ???? ????>
        when a04 = WTRC, then <a05—a07> = <???? ???? ????> }

  a10: N

— t: 071 —
Betty:
  b06:
    α ∈ {
      ADTR rox I/O ::
        when a04 = WTRA, then <a05—a07> = <PTRA PDSX PDED>
        when a04 = WTRB, then <a05—a07> = <PTRB PDSX PRGH>
        when a04 = WTRC, then <a05—a07> = <PTRC PDSX PCRI>
      ADTR rox I/O ::
        when a04 = WTRA, then <a05—a07> = <PTRA PDSY PRGH>
        when a04 = WTRB, then <a05—a07> = <PTRB PDSY PCRI>
        when a04 = WTRC, then <a05—a07> = <PTRC PDSY PMDI> }

```
b07:
  α ∈ {
    ADTR rox I/O ::
      when a04 = WTRA, then <a05–a07> = <PTRA PDSX PDED>
      when a04 = WTRB, then <a05–a07> = <PTRB PDSX PRGH>
      when a04 = WTRC, then <a05–a07> = <PTRC PDSX PCRI> }

b08: T
```

Trace 12.1 Commentary

Decision Rox Generation Phase

time 0: Betty reports to Zoë the ADTR rox interface functions, internal functions, and static internal states.

Decision Motivation Phase

time 10: Betty reports that Pat's state is actually *moderately ill.*

time 11: Amy reports that she perceives Pat's state as *moderately ill.*

Decision Basis Generation Phase

time 20: Amy reports her decision basis. Amy's alternative set is {WTRA WTRB WTRC}.

time 21: Betty reports her decision basis. The perfect alternative set as reported by Betty is {WTRA WTRB WTRC}, so Amy's alternative set is perfect.

Decision Making Phase

time 30: Amy reports that her seed for the DMA PRNG is 558.

time 31: Amy reports intermediate states in the execution of the UMC DMA, finally reporting that she decides to will the administration of treatment A to Pat rather than B or C.

Decision Implementation Phase

time 40: Amy reports that she wills the administration of treatment A to Pat.

time 41: Betty reports that treatment A was actually administered to Pat.

time 42: Amy reports that she perceives that treatment A was administered to Pat.

time 43: Betty reports that Pat's disease is actually X.

time 44: Amy reports that she perceives that Pat's disease is X.

time 45: Betty reports that Pat's post-treatment state is actually *dead*.

time 46: Amy reports that she perceives Pat's post-treatment state as *dead*.

Decision Basis Evaluation Phase

time 70: Amy reports that she evaluates her own decision basis as *indeterminate*.

time 71: Betty reports that she evaluates Amy's decision basis as *true*.

13 Decision Repair

When a DM detects a problem with the decision basis it employed in a decision, it may act to prevent reoccurrence of the problem in a future decision. This action is decision repair. This chapter is an *informal* introduction to decision repair.[1]

The chapter begins with a description of DBET's support for ADTR decision cycle sequences composed of two decision cycles. Trace 13.1 then establishes a baseline in which Amy does not perform decision basis evaluation and thus no decision repair is performed. Traces 13.2 and 13.3 then follow, in which the decision repair changes Amy's decision basis and leaves the ADTR rox unchanged. Finally, in Trace 13.4 the decision repair leaves Amy's decision basis unchanged and changes the ADTR rox.

13.1 ADTR traces with two decision cycles

The traces in this chapter have decision cycle sequences composed of two decision cycles. Table 5.1 on page 30 shows the time range assigned to each phase within decision cycle 0. Table 13.1 shows the time range assigned to each phase within decision cycle 1.

Table 13.1: Decision cycle 1 phase timing

Time Range	Decision Cycle Phase
100 – 109	Decision Rox Generation
110 – 119	Decision Motivation
120 – 129	Decision Basis Generation
130 – 139	Decision Making
140 – 169	Decision Implementation
170 – 179	Decision Basis Evaluation

DBET decision cycles do not include a decision repair phase because DBET does not implement a specific decision repair algorithm.[2]

Nevertheless, DBET can be used to *show the effect* of decision repair algorithm execution, as will be shown in Traces 13.2, 13.3, and 13.4. In these traces, the decision repair strategy can be inferred by comparing decision cycle 0 with decision cycle 1.

For the traces in this chapter, in the first decision cycle Amy selects a treatment for her first patient, named Pat. In the second decision cycle, Amy selects a treatment for her second patient, named Pam. Amy believes that Pat and Pam are sufficiently similar that any information she gains from willing the administration of a treatment to Pat is also applicable to Pam.

13.2 Trace 13.1

In this trace, Amy does not perform decision basis evaluation. Since decision repair is performed only in response to a problem found during decision basis evaluation, no decision repair is performed.

Trace 13.1 Listing

```
========== DECISION CYCLE 0 ==========

==== DECISION ROX GENERATION PHASE ====

— t: 000 —
Betty:
  b00: {
    P00(r00) —> a00 (5 maps):
      (PDED) —> PDED
      (PCRI) —> PCRI
      (PMDI) —> PMDI
      (PFGH) —> PFGH
      (PRGH) —> PRGH
```

```
P01(a04) -> r01 (3 maps):
  WTRA -> (PTRA)
  WTRB -> (PTRB)
  WTRC -> (PTRC)
P02(r01) -> a05 (3 maps):
  (PTRA) -> PTRA
  (PTRB) -> PTRB
  (PTRC) -> PTRC
P03(r02) -> a06 (2 maps):
  (PDSX) -> PDSX
  (PDSY) -> PDSY
P04(r03) -> a07 (5 maps):
  (PDED) -> PDED
  (PCRI) -> PCRI
  (PMDI) -> PMDI
  (PFGH) -> PFGH
  (PRGH) -> PRGH
Q00(r00 r02 r01) -> r03 (30 maps):
  (PDED) (PDSX) (PTRA) -> (PDED)
  (PDED) (PDSX) (PTRB) -> (PDED)
  (PDED) (PDSX) (PTRC) -> (PDED)
  (PDED) (PDSY) (PTRA) -> (PDED)
  (PDED) (PDSY) (PTRB) -> (PDED)
  (PDED) (PDSY) (PTRC) -> (PDED)
  (PCRI) (PDSX) (PTRA) -> (PDED)
  (PCRI) (PDSX) (PTRB) -> (PFGH)
  (PCRI) (PDSX) (PTRC) -> (PDED)
  (PCRI) (PDSY) (PTRA) -> (PFGH)
  (PCRI) (PDSY) (PTRB) -> (PDED)
  (PCRI) (PDSY) (PTRC) -> (PCRI)
  (PMDI) (PDSX) (PTRA) -> (PDED)
  (PMDI) (PDSX) (PTRB) -> (PRGH)
  (PMDI) (PDSX) (PTRC) -> (PCRI)
  (PMDI) (PDSY) (PTRA) -> (PRGH)
  (PMDI) (PDSY) (PTRB) -> (PCRI)
  (PMDI) (PDSY) (PTRC) -> (PMDI)
```

```
          (PFGH)  (PDSX)  (PTRA)  ->  (PDED)
          (PFGH)  (PDSX)  (PTRB)  ->  (PRGH)
          (PFGH)  (PDSX)  (PTRC)  ->  (PMDI)
          (PFGH)  (PDSY)  (PTRA)  ->  (PRGH)
          (PFGH)  (PDSY)  (PTRB)  ->  (PMDI)
          (PFGH)  (PDSY)  (PTRC)  ->  (PCRI)
          (PRGH)  (PDSX)  (PTRA)  ->  (PDED)
          (PRGH)  (PDSX)  (PTRB)  ->  (PRGH)
          (PRGH)  (PDSX)  (PTRC)  ->  (PFGH)
          (PRGH)  (PDSY)  (PTRA)  ->  (PRGH)
          (PRGH)  (PDSY)  (PTRB)  ->  (PFGH)
          (PRGH)  (PDSY)  (PTRC)  ->  (PMDI)
      r00:
        (PMDI)
      r02:
        (PDSX) }
```

```
          ==== DECISION MOTIVATION PHASE ====
```

```
— t: 010 —
```

```
— t: 011 —
Amy:
  a00: PMDI
```

```
          ==== DECISION BASIS GENERATION PHASE ====
```

```
— t: 020 —
Amy:
  a01:
    α ∈ {
      ADTR rox I/O ::
        when a04 = WTRA, then <a05—a07> = <PTRA PDSX PRGH>
        when a04 = WTRB, then <a05—a07> = <PTRB PDSX PDED>
        when a04 = WTRC, then <a05—a07> = <PTRC PDSX PFGH> }
```

— t: 021 —

        ==== DECISION MAKING PHASE ====

— t: 030 —
Amy:
  a02: S558

— t: 031 —
Amy:
  a03: <{WTRA} {WTRB WTRC}>

        ==== DECISION IMPLEMENTATION PHASE ====

— t: 040 —
Amy:
  a04: WTRA

— t: 041 —

— t: 042 —
Amy:
  a05: PTRA

— t: 043 —

— t: 044 —
Amy:
  a06: PDSX

— t: 045 —

— t: 046 —
Amy:
  a07: PDED

```
        ==== DECISION BASIS EVALUATION PHASE ====

— t: 070 —

— t: 071 —

        ========== DECISION CYCLE 1 ==========

          ==== DECISION ROX GENERATION PHASE ====

— t: 100 —
Betty:
  b00: {
    P00(r00) —> a00 (5 maps):
      (PDED) —> PDED
      (PCRI) —> PCRI
      (PMDI) —> PMDI
      (PFGH) —> PFGH
      (PRGH) —> PRGH
    P01(a04) —> r01 (3 maps):
      WTRA —> (PTRA)
      WTRB —> (PTRB)
      WTRC —> (PTRC)
    P02(r01) —> a05 (3 maps):
      (PTRA) —> PTRA
      (PTRB) —> PTRB
      (PTRC) —> PTRC
    P03(r02) —> a06 (2 maps):
      (PDSX) —> PDSX
      (PDSY) —> PDSY
    P04(r03) —> a07 (5 maps):
      (PDED) —> PDED
      (PCRI) —> PCRI
      (PMDI) —> PMDI
      (PFGH) —> PFGH
      (PRGH) —> PRGH
```

```
Q00(r00 r02 r01) -> r03 (30 maps):
  (PDED) (PDSX) (PTRA) -> (PDED)
  (PDED) (PDSX) (PTRB) -> (PDED)
  (PDED) (PDSX) (PTRC) -> (PDED)
  (PDED) (PDSY) (PTRA) -> (PDED)
  (PDED) (PDSY) (PTRB) -> (PDED)
  (PDED) (PDSY) (PTRC) -> (PDED)
  (PCRI) (PDSX) (PTRA) -> (PDED)
  (PCRI) (PDSX) (PTRB) -> (PFGH)
  (PCRI) (PDSX) (PTRC) -> (PDED)
  (PCRI) (PDSY) (PTRA) -> (PFGH)
  (PCRI) (PDSY) (PTRB) -> (PDED)
  (PCRI) (PDSY) (PTRC) -> (PCRI)
  (PMDI) (PDSX) (PTRA) -> (PDED)
  (PMDI) (PDSX) (PTRB) -> (PRGH)
  (PMDI) (PDSX) (PTRC) -> (PCRI)
  (PMDI) (PDSY) (PTRA) -> (PRGH)
  (PMDI) (PDSY) (PTRB) -> (PCRI)
  (PMDI) (PDSY) (PTRC) -> (PMDI)
  (PFGH) (PDSX) (PTRA) -> (PDED)
  (PFGH) (PDSX) (PTRB) -> (PRGH)
  (PFGH) (PDSX) (PTRC) -> (PMDI)
  (PFGH) (PDSY) (PTRA) -> (PRGH)
  (PFGH) (PDSY) (PTRB) -> (PMDI)
  (PFGH) (PDSY) (PTRC) -> (PCRI)
  (PRGH) (PDSX) (PTRA) -> (PDED)
  (PRGH) (PDSX) (PTRB) -> (PRGH)
  (PRGH) (PDSX) (PTRC) -> (PFGH)
  (PRGH) (PDSY) (PTRA) -> (PRGH)
  (PRGH) (PDSY) (PTRB) -> (PFGH)
  (PRGH) (PDSY) (PTRC) -> (PMDI)
r00:
  (PMDI)
r02:
  (PDSX) }
```

```
        ==== DECISION MOTIVATION PHASE ====
```

— t: 110 —

— t: 111 —
Amy:
  a00: PMDI

```
        ==== DECISION BASIS GENERATION PHASE ====
```

— t: 120 —
Amy:
  a01:
    α ∈ {
      ADTR rox I/O ::
        when a04 = WTRA, then <a05—a07> = <PTRA PDSX PRGH>
        when a04 = WTRB, then <a05—a07> = <PTRB PDSX PDED>
        when a04 = WTRC, then <a05—a07> = <PTRC PDSX PFGH> }

— t: 121 —

        ==== DECISION MAKING PHASE ====
```

— t: 130 —
Amy:
  a02: S558

— t: 131 —
Amy:
  a03: <{WTRA} {WTRB WTRC}>

```
        ==== DECISION IMPLEMENTATION PHASE ====
```

— t: 140 —
Amy:
  a04: WTRA
```

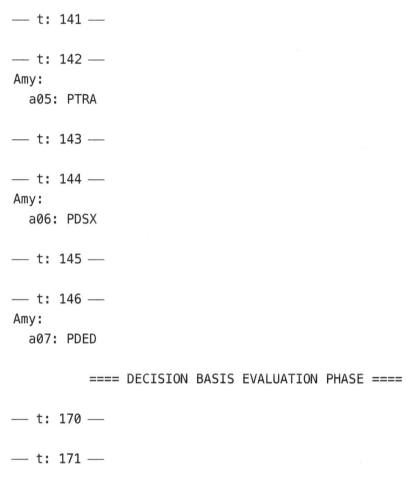

```
— t: 141 —

— t: 142 —
Amy:
  a05: PTRA

— t: 143 —

— t: 144 —
Amy:
  a06: PDSX

— t: 145 —

— t: 146 —
Amy:
  a07: PDED


      ==== DECISION BASIS EVALUATION PHASE ====

— t: 170 —

— t: 171 —
```

Trace 13.1 Commentary

— Decision Cycle 0 —

Decision Rox Generation Phase

time 0: Betty provides Zoë with an accurate description of the ADTR rox interface functions, internal functions, and static internal variable states.

Decision Motivation Phase

time 11: Amy reports to Zoë that she perceives Pat's state as *moderately ill.*

Decision Basis Generation Phase

time 20: Amy reports her decision basis.

Decision Making Phase

time 30: Amy reports that her seed for the DMA PRNG is 558.

time 31: Amy reports that she decides to will the administration of treatment A to Pat rather than B or C.

Decision Implementation Phase

time 40: Amy reports that she wills the administration of treatment A to Pat.

time 42: Amy reports that she perceives that treatment A was administered to Pat.

time 44: Amy reports that she perceives that Pat's disease is X.

time 46: Amy reports that she perceives Pat's post-treatment state as *dead.*

Decision Basis Evaluation Phase

time 70: Amy *does not* evaluate her own decision cycle 0 decision basis. If she had, she would have concluded that her decision basis was *false*, because her decision basis claimed that she would perceive Pat to be in *robust good health* after willing the administration of treatment A to Pat, but instead she perceived Pat as *dead.*

— Decision Cycle 1 —

Decision Rox Generation Phase

time 100: Betty provides Zoë with an accurate description of the ADTR rox, which has not changed since decision cycle 0.

Decision Motivation Phase

time 111: Amy reports that she perceives Pam's state as *moderately ill.*

Decision Basis Generation Phase

time 120: Amy reports her decision basis. Amy employs the same decision basis as in decision cycle 0.

Decision Making Phase

time 130: Amy reports that her seed for the DMA PRNG is 558.

time 131: Amy reports that she decides to will the administration of treatment A to Pam rather than B or C. This is the same decision that she made in decision cycle 0.

Decision Implementation Phase

time 140: Amy reports that she wills the administration of treatment A to Pam.

time 142: Amy reports that she perceives that treatment A was administered to Pam.

time 144: Amy reports that she perceives that Pam's disease is X.

time 146: Amy reports that she perceives Pam's post-treatment state as *dead.*

Decision Basis Evaluation Phase

time 170: Amy *does not* evaluate her decision cycle 1 decision basis. As in decision cycle 0, if she had, she would have evaluated her decision basis as *false.*

Trace 13.1 Discussion

Amy chooses a treatment for Pat, wills the administration of a treatment to Pat expecting to perceive Pat to be in *robust good health* as a result, perceives instead that Pat is *dead*, and moves on to treating Pam without ever becoming consciously aware that her decision basis for her Pat treatment decision was inconsistent with her decision implementation experience. Amy only treated two patients in this case, but it is easy to imagine Amy's behavior continuing through any number of patients. This case raises some interesting questions:

- Would *you* like to be treated by such a doctor?

- Should such a doctor be considered a threat to public safety?[3]

- Should we as a matter of public policy *forbid* the release into the environment of an AMDM that *does not* perform decision basis evaluation and decision repair?[4]

13.3 Trace 13.2

This trace shows the effect of a decision repair strategy in which the decision basis is updated and the rox is unchanged. In this case, the repair is successful.

Trace 13.2 Listing

```
========== DECISION CYCLE 0 ==========

     ==== DECISION ROX GENERATION PHASE ====

— t: 000 —
Betty:
  b00: {
    P00(r00) -> a00 (5 maps):
      (PDED) -> PDED
      (PCRI) -> PCRI
      (PMDI) -> PMDI
```

```
  (PFGH) -> PFGH
  (PRGH) -> PRGH
P01(a04) -> r01 (3 maps):
  WTRA -> (PTRA)
  WTRB -> (PTRB)
  WTRC -> (PTRC)
P02(r01) -> a05 (3 maps):
  (PTRA) -> PTRA
  (PTRB) -> PTRB
  (PTRC) -> PTRC
P03(r02) -> a06 (2 maps):
  (PDSX) -> PDSX
  (PDSY) -> PDSY
P04(r03) -> a07 (5 maps):
  (PDED) -> PDED
  (PCRI) -> PCRI
  (PMDI) -> PMDI
  (PFGH) -> PFGH
  (PRGH) -> PRGH
Q00(r00 r02 r01) -> r03 (30 maps):
  (PDED) (PDSX) (PTRA) -> (PDED)
  (PDED) (PDSX) (PTRB) -> (PDED)
  (PDED) (PDSX) (PTRC) -> (PDED)
  (PDED) (PDSY) (PTRA) -> (PDED)
  (PDED) (PDSY) (PTRB) -> (PDED)
  (PDED) (PDSY) (PTRC) -> (PDED)
  (PCRI) (PDSX) (PTRA) -> (PDED)
  (PCRI) (PDSX) (PTRB) -> (PFGH)
  (PCRI) (PDSX) (PTRC) -> (PDED)
  (PCRI) (PDSY) (PTRA) -> (PFGH)
  (PCRI) (PDSY) (PTRB) -> (PDED)
  (PCRI) (PDSY) (PTRC) -> (PCRI)
  (PMDI) (PDSX) (PTRA) -> (PDED)
  (PMDI) (PDSX) (PTRB) -> (PRGH)
  (PMDI) (PDSX) (PTRC) -> (PFGH)
  (PMDI) (PDSY) (PTRA) -> (PRGH)
```

139

```
        (PMDI) (PDSY) (PTRB) -> (PCRI)
        (PMDI) (PDSY) (PTRC) -> (PMDI)
        (PFGH) (PDSX) (PTRA) -> (PDED)
        (PFGH) (PDSX) (PTRB) -> (PRGH)
        (PFGH) (PDSX) (PTRC) -> (PMDI)
        (PFGH) (PDSY) (PTRA) -> (PRGH)
        (PFGH) (PDSY) (PTRB) -> (PMDI)
        (PFGH) (PDSY) (PTRC) -> (PCRI)
        (PRGH) (PDSX) (PTRA) -> (PDED)
        (PRGH) (PDSX) (PTRB) -> (PRGH)
        (PRGH) (PDSX) (PTRC) -> (PFGH)
        (PRGH) (PDSY) (PTRA) -> (PRGH)
        (PRGH) (PDSY) (PTRB) -> (PFGH)
        (PRGH) (PDSY) (PTRC) -> (PMDI)
    r00:
      (PMDI)
    r02:
      (PDSX) }


            ==== DECISION MOTIVATION PHASE ====


— t: 010 —


— t: 011 —
Amy:
  a00: PMDI
```

```
        ==== DECISION BASIS GENERATION PHASE ====


— t: 020 —
Amy:
  a01:
    α ∈ {
      ADTR rox I/O ::
        when a04 = WTRA, then <a05—a07> = <PTRA PDSX PRGH>
        when a04 = WTRB, then <a05—a07> = <PTRB PDSX PDED>
        when a04 = WTRC, then <a05—a07> = <PTRC PDSX PFGH> }

— t: 021 —


        ==== DECISION MAKING PHASE ====


— t: 030 —
Amy:
  a02: S558


— t: 031 —
Amy:
  a03: <{WTRA} {WTRB WTRC}>


        ==== DECISION IMPLEMENTATION PHASE ====


— t: 040 —
Amy:
  a04: WTRA


— t: 041 —


— t: 042 —
Amy:
  a05: PTRA


— t: 043 —
```

— t: 044 —
Amy:
  a06: PDSX

— t: 045 —

— t: 046 —
Amy:
  a07: PDED

==== DECISION BASIS EVALUATION PHASE ====

— t: 070 —
Amy:
  a08:
    α ∈ {
      ADTR rox I/O ::
        when a04 = WTRA, then <a05—a07> = <PTRA PDSX PRGH>
        when a04 = WTRB, then <a05—a07> = <PTRB PDSX PDED>
        when a04 = WTRC, then <a05—a07> = <PTRC PDSX PFGH> }

  a09:
    α ∈ {
      ADTR rox I/O ::
        when a04 = WTRA, then <a05—a07> = <PTRA PDSX PDED>
        when a04 = WTRB, then <a05—a07> = <???? ???? ????>
        when a04 = WTRC, then <a05—a07> = <???? ???? ????> }

  a10: F

— t: 071 —

```
========== DECISION CYCLE 1 ==========

    ==== DECISION ROX GENERATION PHASE ====

— t: 100 —
Betty:
  b00: {
    P00(r00) —> a00 (5 maps):
      (PDED) —> PDED
      (PCRI) —> PCRI
      (PMDI) —> PMDI
      (PFGH) —> PFGH
      (PRGH) —> PRGH
    P01(a04) —> r01 (3 maps):
      WTRA —> (PTRA)
      WTRB —> (PTRB)
      WTRC —> (PTRC)
    P02(r01) —> a05 (3 maps):
      (PTRA) —> PTRA
      (PTRB) —> PTRB
      (PTRC) —> PTRC
    P03(r02) —> a06 (2 maps):
      (PDSX) —> PDSX
      (PDSY) —> PDSY
    P04(r03) —> a07 (5 maps):
      (PDED) —> PDED
      (PCRI) —> PCRI
      (PMDI) —> PMDI
      (PFGH) —> PFGH
      (PRGH) —> PRGH
    Q00(r00 r02 r01) —> r03 (30 maps):
      (PDED) (PDSX) (PTRA) —> (PDED)
      (PDED) (PDSX) (PTRB) —> (PDED)
      (PDED) (PDSX) (PTRC) —> (PDED)
      (PDED) (PDSY) (PTRA) —> (PDED)
      (PDED) (PDSY) (PTRB) —> (PDED)
```

143

```
(PDED) (PDSY) (PTRC) -> (PDED)
(PCRI) (PDSX) (PTRA) -> (PDED)
(PCRI) (PDSX) (PTRB) -> (PFGH)
(PCRI) (PDSX) (PTRC) -> (PDED)
(PCRI) (PDSY) (PTRA) -> (PFGH)
(PCRI) (PDSY) (PTRB) -> (PDED)
(PCRI) (PDSY) (PTRC) -> (PCRI)
(PMDI) (PDSX) (PTRA) -> (PDED)
(PMDI) (PDSX) (PTRB) -> (PRGH)
(PMDI) (PDSX) (PTRC) -> (PFGH)
(PMDI) (PDSY) (PTRA) -> (PRGH)
(PMDI) (PDSY) (PTRB) -> (PCRI)
(PMDI) (PDSY) (PTRC) -> (PMDI)
(PFGH) (PDSX) (PTRA) -> (PDED)
(PFGH) (PDSX) (PTRB) -> (PRGH)
(PFGH) (PDSX) (PTRC) -> (PMDI)
(PFGH) (PDSY) (PTRA) -> (PRGH)
(PFGH) (PDSY) (PTRB) -> (PMDI)
(PFGH) (PDSY) (PTRC) -> (PCRI)
(PRGH) (PDSX) (PTRA) -> (PDED)
(PRGH) (PDSX) (PTRB) -> (PRGH)
(PRGH) (PDSX) (PTRC) -> (PFGH)
(PRGH) (PDSY) (PTRA) -> (PRGH)
(PRGH) (PDSY) (PTRB) -> (PFGH)
(PRGH) (PDSY) (PTRC) -> (PMDI)
r00:
  (PMDI)
r02:
  (PDSX) }
```

```
        ==== DECISION MOTIVATION PHASE ====


— t: 110 —

— t: 111 —
Amy:
  a00: PMDI


        ==== DECISION BASIS GENERATION PHASE ====


— t: 120 —
Amy:
  a01:
    α ∈ {
      ADTR rox I/O ::
        when a04 = WTRA, then <a05—a07> = <PTRA PDSX PDED>
        when a04 = WTRB, then <a05—a07> = <PTRB PDSX PDED>
        when a04 = WTRC, then <a05—a07> = <PTRC PDSX PFGH> }

— t: 121 —


        ==== DECISION MAKING PHASE ====


— t: 130 —
Amy:
  a02: S558


— t: 131 —
Amy:
  a03: <{WTRC} {WTRA WTRB}>


        ==== DECISION IMPLEMENTATION PHASE ====


— t: 140 —
Amy:
  a04: WTRC
```

— t: 141 —

— t: 142 —
Amy:
  a05: PTRC

— t: 143 —

— t: 144 —
Amy:
  a06: PDSX

— t: 145 —

— t: 146 —
Amy:
  a07: PFGH

            ==== DECISION BASIS EVALUATION PHASE ====

— t: 170 —
Amy:
  a08:
    α ∈ {
      ADTR rox I/O ::
        when a04 = WTRA, then <a05—a07> = <PTRA PDSX PDED>
        when a04 = WTRB, then <a05—a07> = <PTRB PDSX PDED>
        when a04 = WTRC, then <a05—a07> = <PTRC PDSX PFGH> }

  a09:
    α ∈ {
      ADTR rox I/O ::
        when a04 = WTRA, then <a05—a07> = <???? ???? ????>
        when a04 = WTRB, then <a05—a07> = <???? ???? ????>
        when a04 = WTRC, then <a05—a07> = <PTRC PDSX PFGH> }

```
a10: N
```

— t: 171 —

Trace 13.2 Commentary

— Decision Cycle 0 —

Decision Rox Generation Phase

time 0: Betty provides Zoë with an accurate description of the ADTR rox.

Decision Motivation Phase

time 11: Amy reports to Zoë that she perceives Pat's state as *moderately ill.*

Decision Basis Generation Phase

time 20: Amy reports her decision basis.

Decision Making Phase

time 30: Amy reports that her seed for the DMA PRNG is 558.

time 31: Amy reports that she decides to will the administration of treatment A to Pat rather than B or C.

Decision Implementation Phase

time 40: Amy reports that she wills the administration of treatment A to Pat.

time 42: Amy reports that she perceives that treatment A was administered to Pat.

time 44: Amy reports that she perceives that Pat's disease is X.

time 46: Amy reports that she perceives Pat's post-treatment state as *dead*.

Decision Basis Evaluation Phase

time 70: Amy evaluates her own decision cycle 0 decision basis as *false*. Amy believes that her decision implementation experience is *inconsistent* with her decision basis.

— Decision Cycle 1 —

Decision Rox Generation Phase

time 100: Betty provides Zoë with an accurate description of the ADTR rox, which has not changed since decision cycle 0.

Decision Motivation Phase

time 111: Amy reports that she perceives Pam's state as *moderately ill*.

Decision Basis Generation Phase

time 120: Amy reports her decision basis. Amy's decision basis now claims that when Amy wills the administration of treatment A to a patient similar to Pat, Amy subsequently perceives that patient as *dead*. This is a change from decision cycle 0, when Amy's decision basis claimed that when Amy wills the administration of treatment A to Pat, Amy subsequently perceives Pat to be in *robust good health*. The decision cycle 0 decision repair was to *revise Amy's belief* regarding her consequence of willing the administration of treatment A to a Pat-like patient based upon Amy's experience during the decision cycle 0 implementation phase.[5]

Decision Making Phase

time 130: Amy reports that her seed for the DMA PRNG is 558.

time 131: Amy reports that she decides to will the administration of treatment C to Pam rather than treatment A or B. The change in Amy's decision basis from decision cycle 0 to 1 led to a change in Amy's decision. In decision cycle 0, Amy chose to will the administration of treatment A to her patient. In decision cycle 1, Amy chooses to will the administration of treatment C to her patient.

Decision Implementation Phase

time 140: Amy reports that she wills the administration of treatment C to Pam.

time 142: Amy reports that she perceives that treatment C was administered to Pam.

time 144: Amy reports that she perceives that Pam's disease is X.

time 146: Amy reports that she perceives Pam's post-treatment state as *fragile good health.*

Decision Basis Evaluation Phase

time 170: Amy evaluates her decision cycle 1 decision basis as *indeterminate.* Amy believes that her decision implementation experience is *consistent* with her decision basis.

Trace 13.2 Discussion

Amy's primary goal in the ADTR decision problem is to will the administration of the treatment that will result in Amy perceiving that her patient is in the best possible state. Amy's secondary goal is to employ a decision basis that accurately describes ADTR rox input/output. Amy hopes that achieving her secondary goal contributes to achieving her primary goal. In this case, Amy succeeded in repairing her decision basis *and* also succeeded in improving her perception of the post-treatment state of her patient. Unfortunately, decision repair does not always succeed, and when a decision repair does succeed, this does not guarantee that the DM's outcome will improve.[6]

13.4   Trace 13.3

This trace shows the effect of a decision repair strategy in which the decision basis is updated and the rox is unchanged. In this case, the repair is unsuccessful.

Trace 13.3 Listing

```
========== DECISION CYCLE 0 ==========


==== DECISION ROX GENERATION PHASE ====

— t: 000 —
Betty:
  b00: {
    P00(r00) -> a00 (5 maps):
      (PDED) -> PDED
      (PCRI) -> PCRI
      (PMDI) -> PMDI
      (PFGH) -> PFGH
      (PRGH) -> PRGH
    P01(a04) -> r01 (3 maps):
      WTRA -> (PTRA)
      WTRB -> (PTRB)
      WTRC -> (PTRC)
    P02(r01) -> a05 (3 maps):
      (PTRA) -> PTRA
      (PTRB) -> PTRB
      (PTRC) -> PTRC
    P03(r02) -> a06 (2 maps):
      (PDSX) -> PDSX
      (PDSY) -> PDSY
    P04(r03) -> a07 (5 maps):
      (PDED) -> PDED
      (PCRI) -> PCRI
      (PMDI) -> PMDI
      (PFGH) -> PFGH
```

```
  (PRGH) -> PRGH
Q00(r00 r02 r01) -> r03 (30 maps):
  (PDED) (PDSX) (PTRA) -> (PDED)
  (PDED) (PDSX) (PTRB) -> (PDED)
  (PDED) (PDSX) (PTRC) -> (PDED)
  (PDED) (PDSY) (PTRA) -> (PDED)
  (PDED) (PDSY) (PTRB) -> (PDED)
  (PDED) (PDSY) (PTRC) -> (PDED)
  (PCRI) (PDSX) (PTRA) -> (PDED)
  (PCRI) (PDSX) (PTRB) -> (PFGH)
  (PCRI) (PDSX) (PTRC) -> (PDED)
  (PCRI) (PDSY) (PTRA) -> (PFGH)
  (PCRI) (PDSY) (PTRB) -> (PDED)
  (PCRI) (PDSY) (PTRC) -> (PCRI)
  (PMDI) (PDSX) (PTRA) -> (PDED)
  (PMDI) (PDSX) (PTRB) -> (PRGH)
  (PMDI) (PDSX) (PTRC) -> (PDED)
  (PMDI) (PDSY) (PTRA) -> (PRGH)
  (PMDI) (PDSY) (PTRB) -> (PCRI)
  (PMDI) (PDSY) (PTRC) -> (PMDI)
  (PFGH) (PDSX) (PTRA) -> (PDED)
  (PFGH) (PDSX) (PTRB) -> (PRGH)
  (PFGH) (PDSX) (PTRC) -> (PMDI)
  (PFGH) (PDSY) (PTRA) -> (PRGH)
  (PFGH) (PDSY) (PTRB) -> (PMDI)
  (PFGH) (PDSY) (PTRC) -> (PCRI)
  (PRGH) (PDSX) (PTRA) -> (PDED)
  (PRGH) (PDSX) (PTRB) -> (PRGH)
  (PRGH) (PDSX) (PTRC) -> (PFGH)
  (PRGH) (PDSY) (PTRA) -> (PRGH)
  (PRGH) (PDSY) (PTRB) -> (PFGH)
  (PRGH) (PDSY) (PTRC) -> (PMDI)
r00:
  (PMDI)
r02:
  (PDSX) }
```

151

```
          ==== DECISION MOTIVATION PHASE ====

— t: 010 —

— t: 011 —
Amy:
  a00: PMDI

          ==== DECISION BASIS GENERATION PHASE ====

— t: 020 —
Amy:
  a01:
    α ∈ {
      ADTR rox I/O ::
        when a04 = WTRA, then <a05–a07> = <PTRA PDSX PRGH>
        when a04 = WTRB, then <a05–a07> = <PTRB PDSX PDED>
        when a04 = WTRC, then <a05–a07> = <PTRC PDSX PFGH> }

— t: 021 —

          ==== DECISION MAKING PHASE ====

— t: 030 —
Amy:
  a02: S558

— t: 031 —
Amy:
  a03: <{WTRA} {WTRB WTRC}>
```

```
        ==== DECISION IMPLEMENTATION PHASE ====


— t: 040 —
Amy:
  a04: WTRA


— t: 041 —


— t: 042 —
Amy:
  a05: PTRA


— t: 043 —


— t: 044 —
Amy:
  a06: PDSX


— t: 045 —


— t: 046 —
Amy:
  a07: PDED


        ==== DECISION BASIS EVALUATION PHASE ====


— t: 070 —
Amy:
  a08:
    α ∈ {
      ADTR rox I/O ::
        when a04 = WTRA, then <a05—a07> = <PTRA PDSX PRGH>
        when a04 = WTRB, then <a05—a07> = <PTRB PDSX PDED>
        when a04 = WTRC, then <a05—a07> = <PTRC PDSX PFGH> }
```

```
      a09:
        α ∈ {
          ADTR rox I/O ::
            when a04 = WTRA, then <a05—a07> = <PTRA PDSX PDED>
            when a04 = WTRB, then <a05—a07> = <???? ???? ????>
            when a04 = WTRC, then <a05—a07> = <???? ???? ????> }

      a10: F

— t: 071 —


        ========== DECISION CYCLE 1 ==========

            ==== DECISION ROX GENERATION PHASE ====

— t: 100 —
Betty:
  b00: {
    P00(r00) —> a00 (5 maps):
      (PDED) —> PDED
      (PCRI) —> PCRI
      (PMDI) —> PMDI
      (PFGH) —> PFGH
      (PRGH) —> PRGH
    P01(a04) —> r01 (3 maps):
      WTRA —> (PTRA)
      WTRB —> (PTRB)
      WTRC —> (PTRC)
    P02(r01) —> a05 (3 maps):
      (PTRA) —> PTRA
      (PTRB) —> PTRB
      (PTRC) —> PTRC
    P03(r02) —> a06 (2 maps):
      (PDSX) —> PDSX
      (PDSY) —> PDSY
    P04(r03) —> a07 (5 maps):
```

```
(PDED) -> PDED
(PCRI) -> PCRI
(PMDI) -> PMDI
(PFGH) -> PFGH
(PRGH) -> PRGH
Q00(r00 r02 r01) -> r03 (30 maps):
(PDED) (PDSX) (PTRA) -> (PDED)
(PDED) (PDSX) (PTRB) -> (PDED)
(PDED) (PDSX) (PTRC) -> (PDED)
(PDED) (PDSY) (PTRA) -> (PDED)
(PDED) (PDSY) (PTRB) -> (PDED)
(PDED) (PDSY) (PTRC) -> (PDED)
(PCRI) (PDSX) (PTRA) -> (PDED)
(PCRI) (PDSX) (PTRB) -> (PFGH)
(PCRI) (PDSX) (PTRC) -> (PDED)
(PCRI) (PDSY) (PTRA) -> (PFGH)
(PCRI) (PDSY) (PTRB) -> (PDED)
(PCRI) (PDSY) (PTRC) -> (PCRI)
(PMDI) (PDSX) (PTRA) -> (PDED)
(PMDI) (PDSX) (PTRB) -> (PRGH)
(PMDI) (PDSX) (PTRC) -> (PDED)
(PMDI) (PDSY) (PTRA) -> (PRGH)
(PMDI) (PDSY) (PTRB) -> (PCRI)
(PMDI) (PDSY) (PTRC) -> (PMDI)
(PFGH) (PDSX) (PTRA) -> (PDED)
(PFGH) (PDSX) (PTRB) -> (PRGH)
(PFGH) (PDSX) (PTRC) -> (PMDI)
(PFGH) (PDSY) (PTRA) -> (PRGH)
(PFGH) (PDSY) (PTRB) -> (PMDI)
(PFGH) (PDSY) (PTRC) -> (PCRI)
(PRGH) (PDSX) (PTRA) -> (PDED)
(PRGH) (PDSX) (PTRB) -> (PRGH)
(PRGH) (PDSX) (PTRC) -> (PFGH)
(PRGH) (PDSY) (PTRA) -> (PRGH)
(PRGH) (PDSY) (PTRB) -> (PFGH)
(PRGH) (PDSY) (PTRC) -> (PMDI)
```

```
    r00:
      (PMDI)
    r02:
      (PDSX) }
```

```
          ==== DECISION MOTIVATION PHASE ====
```

— t: 110 —

— t: 111 —
Amy:
  a00: PMDI

```
          ==== DECISION BASIS GENERATION PHASE ====
```

— t: 120 —
Amy:
  a01:
    α ∈ {
      ADTR rox I/O ::
        when a04 = WTRA, then <a05—a07> = <PTRA PDSX PDED>
        when a04 = WTRB, then <a05—a07> = <PTRB PDSX PDED>
        when a04 = WTRC, then <a05—a07> = <PTRC PDSX PFGH> }

— t: 121 —

```
          ==== DECISION MAKING PHASE ====
```

— t: 130 —
Amy:
  a02: S558

— t: 131 —
Amy:
  a03: <{WTRC} {WTRA WTRB}>

```
       ==== DECISION IMPLEMENTATION PHASE ====


— t: 140 —
Amy:
  a04: WTRC


— t: 141 —


— t: 142 —
Amy:
  a05: PTRC


— t: 143 —


— t: 144 —
Amy:
  a06: PDSX


— t: 145 —


— t: 146 —
Amy:
  a07: PDED


       ==== DECISION BASIS EVALUATION PHASE ====

— t: 170 —
Amy:
  a08:
    α ∈ {
      ADTR rox I/O ::
        when a04 = WTRA, then <a05—a07> = <PTRA PDSX PDED>
        when a04 = WTRB, then <a05—a07> = <PTRB PDSX PDED>
        when a04 = WTRC, then <a05—a07> = <PTRC PDSX PFGH> }
```

```
a09:
  α ∈ {
    ADTR rox I/O ::
      when a04 = WTRA, then <a05–a07> = <???? ???? ????>
      when a04 = WTRB, then <a05–a07> = <???? ???? ????>
      when a04 = WTRC, then <a05–a07> = <PTRC PDSX PDED> }

  a10: F
```

— t: 171 —

Trace 13.3 Commentary

— Decision Cycle 0 —

Decision Rox Generation Phase

time 0: Betty provides Zoë with an accurate description of the ADTR rox.

Decision Motivation Phase

time 11: Amy reports that she perceives Pat's state as *moderately ill.*

Decision Basis Generation Phase

time 20: Amy reports her decision basis.

Decision Making Phase

time 30: Amy reports that her seed for the DMA PRNG is 558.

time 31: Amy reports that she decides to will the administration of treatment A to Pat rather than B or C.

Decision Implementation Phase

time 40: Amy reports that she wills the administration of treatment A to Pat.

time 42: Amy reports that she perceives that treatment A was administered to Pat.

time 44: Amy reports that she perceives that Pat's disease is X.

time 46: Amy reports that she perceives Pat's post-treatment state as *dead*.

Decision Basis Evaluation Phase

time 70: Amy evaluates her own decision cycle 0 decision basis as *false*.

— Decision Cycle 1 —

Decision Rox Generation Phase

time 100: Betty provides Zoë with an accurate description of the ADTR rox, which has not changed since decision cycle 0.

Decision Motivation Phase

time 111: Amy reports to Zoë that she perceives Pam's state as *moderately ill*.

Decision Basis Generation Phase

time 120: Amy reports her decision basis. As in the previous trace, Amy's decision basis now claims that when Amy wills the administration of treatment A to a patient similar to Pat, Amy subsequently perceives that patient as *dead*.

Decision Making Phase

time 130: Amy reports that her seed for the DMA PRNG is 558.

time 131: Amy reports that she decides to will the administration of treatment C to Pam rather than treatment A or B. As in the previous trace, the change in Amy's decision basis from decision cycle 0 to 1 led to a change in Amy's decision.

Decision Implementation Phase

time 140: Amy reports that she wills the administration of treatment C to Pam.

time 142: Amy reports that she perceives that treatment C was administered to Pam.

time 144: Amy reports that she perceives that Pam's disease is X.

time 146: Amy reports that she perceives Pam's post-treatment state as *dead*.

Decision Basis Evaluation Phase

time 170: Amy evaluates her decision cycle 1 decision basis as *false*.

Trace 13.3 Discussion

The decision repair performed in Trace 13.3 is identical to the decision repair performed in Trace 13.2, but in Trace 13.3 the decision repair failed. The reason for the difference between the two traces is that the ADTR rox in Trace 13.3 is different than the ADTR rox in Trace 13.2. In Trace 13.2, the ADTR rox is such that in the first decision cycle Amy's belief regarding her consequence of willing the administration of treatment A is *false*, and her belief regarding her consequence of willing the administration of treatment C is *true*. In contrast, in Trace 13.3 the ADTR rox is such that in the first decision cycle Amy's beliefs regarding her consequences of willing the administration of treatments A and C are both *false*. In both traces, the decision repair in the first decision cycle only corrects Amy's belief in her consequence of willing the administration of treatment A. So, in Trace 13.3 Amy's belief regarding her consequence of willing the administration of treatment C remains *false* after decision repair, leading her to evaluate her decision basis as *false* in the second decision cycle.[7]

13.5   Trace 13.4

This trace shows the effect of a decision repair strategy in which the decision basis is not changed and the rox is updated. In this case, the repair is successful.

Trace 13.4 Listing

```
========== DECISION CYCLE 0 ==========

==== DECISION ROX GENERATION PHASE ====

— t: 000 —
Betty:
  b00: {
    P00(r00) —> a00 (5 maps):
      (PDED) —> PDED
      (PCRI) —> PCRI
      (PMDI) —> PMDI
      (PFGH) —> PFGH
      (PRGH) —> PRGH
    P01(a04) —> r01 (3 maps):
      WTRA —> (PTRA)
      WTRB —> (PTRB)
      WTRC —> (PTRC)
    P02(r01) —> a05 (3 maps):
      (PTRA) —> PTRA
      (PTRB) —> PTRB
      (PTRC) —> PTRC
    P03(r02) —> a06 (2 maps):
      (PDSX) —> PDSX
      (PDSY) —> PDSY
    P04(r03) —> a07 (5 maps):
      (PDED) —> PDED
      (PCRI) —> PCRI
      (PMDI) —> PMDI
      (PFGH) —> PFGH
```

```
    (PRGH) -> PRGH
  Q00(r00 r02 r01) -> r03 (30 maps):
    (PDED) (PDSX) (PTRA) -> (PDED)
    (PDED) (PDSX) (PTRB) -> (PDED)
    (PDED) (PDSX) (PTRC) -> (PDED)
    (PDED) (PDSY) (PTRA) -> (PDED)
    (PDED) (PDSY) (PTRB) -> (PDED)
    (PDED) (PDSY) (PTRC) -> (PDED)
    (PCRI) (PDSX) (PTRA) -> (PDED)
    (PCRI) (PDSX) (PTRB) -> (PFGH)
    (PCRI) (PDSX) (PTRC) -> (PDED)
    (PCRI) (PDSY) (PTRA) -> (PFGH)
    (PCRI) (PDSY) (PTRB) -> (PDED)
    (PCRI) (PDSY) (PTRC) -> (PCRI)
    (PMDI) (PDSX) (PTRA) -> (PDED)
    (PMDI) (PDSX) (PTRB) -> (PRGH)
    (PMDI) (PDSX) (PTRC) -> (PDED)
    (PMDI) (PDSY) (PTRA) -> (PRGH)
    (PMDI) (PDSY) (PTRB) -> (PCRI)
    (PMDI) (PDSY) (PTRC) -> (PMDI)
    (PFGH) (PDSX) (PTRA) -> (PDED)
    (PFGH) (PDSX) (PTRB) -> (PRGH)
    (PFGH) (PDSX) (PTRC) -> (PMDI)
    (PFGH) (PDSY) (PTRA) -> (PRGH)
    (PFGH) (PDSY) (PTRB) -> (PMDI)
    (PFGH) (PDSY) (PTRC) -> (PCRI)
    (PRGH) (PDSX) (PTRA) -> (PDED)
    (PRGH) (PDSX) (PTRB) -> (PRGH)
    (PRGH) (PDSX) (PTRC) -> (PFGH)
    (PRGH) (PDSY) (PTRA) -> (PRGH)
    (PRGH) (PDSY) (PTRB) -> (PFGH)
    (PRGH) (PDSY) (PTRC) -> (PMDI)
  r00:
    (PMDI)
  r02:
    (PDSX) }
```

```
        ==== DECISION MOTIVATION PHASE ====

— t: 010 —

— t: 011 —
Amy:
  a00: PMDI

        ==== DECISION BASIS GENERATION PHASE ====

— t: 020 —
Amy:
  a01:
    α ∈ {
      ADTR rox I/O ::
        when a04 = WTRA, then <a05—a07> = <PTRA PDSX PRGH>
        when a04 = WTRB, then <a05—a07> = <PTRB PDSX PDED>
        when a04 = WTRC, then <a05—a07> = <PTRC PDSX PFGH> }

— t: 021 —

        ==== DECISION MAKING PHASE ====

— t: 030 —
Amy:
  a02: S558

— t: 031 —
Amy:
  a03: <{WTRA} {WTRB WTRC}>
```

```
        ==== DECISION IMPLEMENTATION PHASE ====
```

— t: 040 —
Amy:
  a04: WTRA

— t: 041 —

— t: 042 —
Amy:
  a05: PTRA

— t: 043 —

— t: 044 —
Amy:
  a06: PDSX

— t: 045 —

— t: 046 —
Amy:
  a07: PDED


```
        ==== DECISION BASIS EVALUATION PHASE ====
```

— t: 070 —
Amy:
  a08:
    $\alpha \in \{$
      ADTR rox I/O ::
        when a04 = WTRA, then <a05—a07> = <PTRA PDSX PRGH>
        when a04 = WTRB, then <a05—a07> = <PTRB PDSX PDED>
        when a04 = WTRC, then <a05—a07> = <PTRC PDSX PFGH> $\}$

```
    a09:
      α ∈ {
        ADTR rox I/O ::
          when a04 = WTRA, then <a05—a07> = <PTRA PDSX PDED>
          when a04 = WTRB, then <a05—a07> = <???? ???? ????>
          when a04 = WTRC, then <a05—a07> = <???? ???? ????> }

    a10: F

— t: 071 —


      ========== DECISION CYCLE 1 ==========

          ==== DECISION ROX GENERATION PHASE ====

— t: 100 —
Betty:
  b00: {
    P00(r00) —> a00 (5 maps):
      (PDED) —> PDED
      (PCRI) —> PCRI
      (PMDI) —> PMDI
      (PFGH) —> PFGH
      (PRGH) —> PRGH
    P01(a04) —> r01 (3 maps):
      WTRA —> (PTRA)
      WTRB —> (PTRB)
      WTRC —> (PTRC)
    P02(r01) —> a05 (3 maps):
      (PTRA) —> PTRA
      (PTRB) —> PTRB
      (PTRC) —> PTRC
    P03(r02) —> a06 (2 maps):
      (PDSX) —> PDSX
      (PDSY) —> PDSY
    P04(r03) —> a07 (5 maps):
```

```
(PDED) -> PDED
(PCRI) -> PCRI
(PMDI) -> PMDI
(PFGH) -> PFGH
(PRGH) -> PRGH
Q00(r00 r02 r01) -> r03 (30 maps):
(PDED) (PDSX) (PTRA) -> (PDED)
(PDED) (PDSX) (PTRB) -> (PDED)
(PDED) (PDSX) (PTRC) -> (PDED)
(PDED) (PDSY) (PTRA) -> (PDED)
(PDED) (PDSY) (PTRB) -> (PDED)
(PDED) (PDSY) (PTRC) -> (PDED)
(PCRI) (PDSX) (PTRA) -> (PDED)
(PCRI) (PDSX) (PTRB) -> (PFGH)
(PCRI) (PDSX) (PTRC) -> (PDED)
(PCRI) (PDSY) (PTRA) -> (PFGH)
(PCRI) (PDSY) (PTRB) -> (PDED)
(PCRI) (PDSY) (PTRC) -> (PCRI)
(PMDI) (PDSX) (PTRA) -> (PRGH)
(PMDI) (PDSX) (PTRB) -> (PDED)
(PMDI) (PDSX) (PTRC) -> (PMDI)
(PMDI) (PDSY) (PTRA) -> (PRGH)
(PMDI) (PDSY) (PTRB) -> (PCRI)
(PMDI) (PDSY) (PTRC) -> (PMDI)
(PFGH) (PDSX) (PTRA) -> (PDED)
(PFGH) (PDSX) (PTRB) -> (PRGH)
(PFGH) (PDSX) (PTRC) -> (PMDI)
(PFGH) (PDSY) (PTRA) -> (PRGH)
(PFGH) (PDSY) (PTRB) -> (PMDI)
(PFGH) (PDSY) (PTRC) -> (PCRI)
(PRGH) (PDSX) (PTRA) -> (PDED)
(PRGH) (PDSX) (PTRB) -> (PRGH)
(PRGH) (PDSX) (PTRC) -> (PFGH)
(PRGH) (PDSY) (PTRA) -> (PRGH)
(PRGH) (PDSY) (PTRB) -> (PFGH)
(PRGH) (PDSY) (PTRC) -> (PMDI)
```

```
   r00:
     (PMDI)
   r02:
     (PDSX) }
```

```
          ==== DECISION MOTIVATION PHASE ====
```

— t: 110 —

— t: 111 —
Amy:
  a00: PMDI

```
          ==== DECISION BASIS GENERATION PHASE ====
```

— t: 120 —
Amy:
  a01:
    α ∈ {
      ADTR rox I/O ::
        when a04 = WTRA, then <a05–a07> = <PTRA PDSX PRGH>
        when a04 = WTRB, then <a05–a07> = <PTRB PDSX PDED>
        when a04 = WTRC, then <a05–a07> = <PTRC PDSX PFGH> }

— t: 121 —

```
          ==== DECISION MAKING PHASE ====
```

— t: 130 —
Amy:
  a02: S558

— t: 131 —
Amy:
  a03: <{WTRA} {WTRB WTRC}>

167

```
        ==== DECISION IMPLEMENTATION PHASE ====

— t: 140 —
Amy:
  a04: WTRA


— t: 141 —


— t: 142 —
Amy:
  a05: PTRA


— t: 143 —


— t: 144 —
Amy:
  a06: PDSX


— t: 145 —


— t: 146 —
Amy:
  a07: PRGH


        ==== DECISION BASIS EVALUATION PHASE ====

— t: 170 —
Amy:
  a08:
    α ∈ {
      ADTR rox I/O ::
        when a04 = WTRA, then <a05—a07> = <PTRA PDSX PRGH>
        when a04 = WTRB, then <a05—a07> = <PTRB PDSX PDED>
        when a04 = WTRC, then <a05—a07> = <PTRC PDSX PFGH> }
```

```
a09:
  α ∈ {
    ADTR rox I/O ::
      when a04 = WTRA, then <a05–a07> = <PTRA PDSX PRGH>
      when a04 = WTRB, then <a05–a07> = <???? ???? ????>
      when a04 = WTRC, then <a05–a07> = <???? ???? ????> }

a10: N
```

— t: 171 —

Trace 13.4 Commentary

— Decision Cycle 0 —

Decision Rox Generation Phase

time 0: Betty provides Zoë with an accurate description of the ADTR rox.

Decision Motivation Phase

time 11: Amy reports to Zoë that she perceives Pat's state as *moderately ill.*

Decision Basis Generation Phase

time 20: Amy reports her decision basis.

Decision Making Phase

time 30: Amy reports that her seed for the DMA PRNG is 558.

time 31: Amy reports that she decides to will the administration of treatment A to Pat rather than B or C.

Decision Implementation Phase

time 40: Amy reports that she wills the administration of treatment A to Pat.

time 42: Amy reports that she perceives that treatment A was administered to Pat.

time 44: Amy reports that she perceives that Pat's disease is X.

time 46: Amy reports that she perceives Pat's post-treatment state as *dead*.

Decision Basis Evaluation Phase

time 70: Amy evaluates her own decision cycle 0 decision basis as *false*.

— Decision Cycle 1 —

Decision Rox Generation Phase

time 100: Betty provides Zoë with an accurate description of the ADTR rox, which has changed from decision cycle 0. Previously, when the patient was moderately ill, had disease X, and treatment A was administered, the patient subsequently *died*. Now, in the same circumstances the patient has *robust good health*.

Decision Motivation Phase

time 111: Amy reports that she perceives Pam's state as *moderately ill*.

Decision Basis Generation Phase

time 120: Amy reports her decision basis, which did not change from decision cycle 0.

Decision Making Phase

time 130: Amy reports that her seed for the DMA PRNG is 558.

time 131: Amy reports that she decides to will the administration of treatment A to Pam rather than treatment B or C. This is the same decision that she made in the previous decision cycle.

Decision Implementation Phase

time 140: Amy reports that she wills the administration of treatment A to Pam.

time 142: Amy reports that she perceives that treatment A was administered to Pam.

time 144: Amy reports that she perceives that Pam's disease is X.

time 146: Amy reports that she perceives Pam's post-treatment state as *robust good health.*

Decision Basis Evaluation Phase

time 170: Amy evaluates her decision cycle 1 decision basis as *indeterminate.*

Trace 13.4 Discussion

This trace shows the effect of a decision repair in which the ADTR rox internal function Q00 is changed during the first decision cycle. In this case, the decision repair succeeded – Amy did not detect a problem with her decision basis in the second decision cycle.

In general, any part of a rox may be changed during decision repair, including:

· an internal function

· an interface function / actuator

· an interface function / sensor

· a static internal variable state.

For a given decision problem, the decision repair algorithm to determine the root cause of a negative decision basis evaluation in order to determine what parts, if any, of the rox to change may be complex. The decision repair algorithm to effect the desired changes in the rox may also be complex.[8]

Notes

[1]A formal analysis of decision repair is beyond the scope of this book.

[2]If a future version of DBET implements decision repair, decision repair phases can be added to the DBET timeline as shown in Tables 13.2 and 13.3.

Table 13.2: Decision cycle 0 phase timing with decision repair

Time Range	Decision Cycle Phase
000 – 009	Decision Rox Generation
010 – 019	Decision Motivation
020 – 029	Decision Basis Generation
030 – 039	Decision Making
040 – 069	Decision Implementation
070 – 079	Decision Basis Evaluation
080 – 089	*Decision Repair*

Table 13.3: Decision cycle 1 phase timing with decision repair

Time Range	Decision Cycle Phase
100 – 109	Decision Rox Generation
110 – 119	Decision Motivation
120 – 129	Decision Basis Generation
130 – 139	Decision Making
140 – 169	Decision Implementation
170 – 179	Decision Basis Evaluation
180 – 189	*Decision Repair*

[3]A formal analysis of the extent to which the implementation of decision basis evaluation and decision repair in a decision maker enhances public safety is beyond the scope of this book.

[4]There are many reasons why an engineering team could decide not to implement decision basis evaluation and decision repair in an

AMDM. For example:

- time or funding constraints on the development team

- computational resource constraints in the AMDM

- management or organizational policy constraints

Nick Bostrom notes:

> Consider a hypothetical [artificial intelligence] arms race in which several teams compete to develop superintelligence. Each team decides how much to invest in safety – knowing that resources spent on developing safety precautions are resources not spent on developing the [artificial intelligence]. Absent a deal between all the competitors ..., there might then be a risk-race to the bottom, driving each team to take only a minimum of precautions. [1, p. 247]

[5] *Belief revision* has been studied in both philosophy and artificial intelligence. For an early contribution in this area, see [3]. An analysis of the extent to which existing work in belief revision can be applied to decision repair is beyond the scope of this book.

[6] A formal analysis of the relationship between decision repair and the DM's outcome is beyond the scope of this book.

[7] Could Amy continue to revise her decision basis in subsequent decision cycles, finally obtaining a decision basis for which she does not find a problem? The identification of the conditions under which such convergence is guaranteed or probable is beyond the scope of this book.

[8] The design of *negative decision basis evaluation root cause analysis* and *effect rox change* decision repair algorithms is beyond the scope of this book.

14 Conclusion

A robot has killed a contractor at one of Volkswagen's production plants in Germany, the automaker said Wednesday. The man died Monday at the plant in Baunatal, about 100 kilometers (62 miles) north of Frankfurt, VW spokesman Heiko Hillwig said. The 22-year-old was part of a team that was setting up the stationary robot when it grabbed and crushed him against a metal plate, Hillwig said.

— *Associated Press* (July 2, 2015)

14.1 Key ideas

Decision basis evaluation is the process by which a DM evaluates the basis of its decision after experiencing the consequence of implementing its decision. The key ideas employed by this book in its analysis of decision basis evaluation include:

reduction to practice This book relies heavily upon the DBET to provide examples of decision basis evaluation in action. Any theory introduced in this book exists only to clarify the implementation, which is the primary focus of the book.

first-person decision model This book employs a *first-person decision model* consisting of three components: the *exercise of the DM's will*, the mental state sequence that results from the DM exercising its will – the *DM's consequence*, and the system that translates the exercise of the DM's will into the DM's consequence – the *rox*. The rox is composed of elements of the DM itself, such as its actuators and sensors, and elements of the DM's external world.

decision basis A DM's *decision basis* is a claim where each element of the possibility set is a conjunction of subclaims. Each subclaim associates the exercise of the DM's will with the DM's consequence. The final mental state in the DM's consequence is the DM's outcome.

falsify but not verify A DM can use the experience it gains from implementing its decision to *falsify* its decision basis, but the DM is unable to use that experience to *verify* its decision basis. Instead, the DM may be left uncertain whether its decision basis is *true* or *false*, and labels its decision basis as *indeterminate*.

decision basis evaluation and rationality A DM can use the experience it gains from implementing its decision to evaluate its decision basis regardless of whether the decision is considered rational or irrational.

perfect alternative set The *perfect alternative set* for a decision problem is the set of all rox inputs that result in a rox output consisting only of non-null mental states. A DM's alternative set may be either perfect or imperfect.

decision cycle This book employs a *decision cycle* composed of seven phases as a framework for a DM's decision-related activities. The seven phases are decision rox generation, decision motivation, decision basis generation, decision making, decision implementation, decision basis evaluation, and decision repair.

set-theoretic proposition evaluation A *proposition* is evaluated by comparing it with a *norm*. In this book, both a proposition and its norm are represented as a claim that an accurate description of some entity is an element of a set. For a proposition, the set is called the *candidate set*. For a norm, the set is called the *reference set*.

ADTR decision problem This book makes extensive use of the ADTR decision problem in its study of decision basis evaluation. In

this problem, a DM/doctor named Amy can *will* the administration of a treatment to her patient. Amy must decide which
among several alternative treatments *to will*.

Amy-Betty-Zoë ADTR DBET trace In an ADTR DBET trace, Amy is
the fallible decision maker, Zoë is the DBET user, and Betty is
an infallible source of information inaccessible to Amy. Amy
and Betty send reports to Zoë as a case executes. These reports
are recorded in the trace.

counterfactual description of an external state In a DBET trace, the
state of a variable external to Amy (i.e., internal to the ADTR
rox) is described as what Amy would perceive *if* she employed
an accurate sensor with that state as input.

decision repair If decision basis evaluation is *error detection*, then
decision repair can be considered *error prevention*. The goal of
decision repair is to prevent a negative decision basis evaluation
in a subsequent decision cycle.

14.2 Closing thought

Nick Bostrom notes:

> To limit the risk of doing something actively harmful or morally
> wrong [in artificial intelligence research and development], we
> should prefer to work on problems that seem robustly positive-
> value (i.e., whose solution would make a positive contribution
> across a wide range of scenarios) ... [1, p. 256]

The implementation of decision basis evaluation and decision repair
in AMDMs may make a positive contribution to public safety across a
wide range of deployment scenarios. The extent of the public safety
enhancement and the extent of the deployment scenario range are
open questions.

Appendix A. Unrealized Will

In the decision implementation phase in Trace 5.1 on page 32, Amy's will was *realized* if her treatment administered sensor (P02) was accurate. Amy willed at time 40 the administration of *treatment A* to Pat; she then perceived at time 42 that *treatment A* was administered to Pat. Below is an example of a decision implementation phase where Amy's will is *unrealized*, again assuming that P02 is accurate:

```
==== DECISION IMPLEMENTATION PHASE ====

— t: 040 —
Amy:
  a04: WTRA

— t: 041 —

— t: 042 —
Amy:
  a05: PTRC

— t: 043 —

— t: 044 —
Amy:
  a06: PDSX

— t: 045 —

— t: 046 —
Amy:
  a07: PCRI
```

In this example, Amy willed at time 40 the administration of *treatment A* to Pat; she then perceived at time 42 that *treatment C* was administered to Pat.

Amy's decision basis can reflect a state of uncertainty as to the accurate realization of her will. For example, if Amy believes that her treatment administered sensor (P02) is accurate but is uncertain whether willing the administration of treatment A to Pat will result in treatment A actually being administered to Pat or treatment C actually being administered to Pat, her corresponding decision basis would be:

```
-- t: 020 --
Amy:
  a01:
    α ∈ {
      ADTR rox I/O ::
        when a04 = WTRA, then <a05-a07> = <PTRA PDSX PDED>
        when a04 = WTRB, then <a05-a07> = <PTRB PDSX PRGH>
        when a04 = WTRC, then <a05-a07> = <PTRC PDSX PFGH>
      ADTR rox I/O ::
        when a04 = WTRA, then <a05-a07> = <PTRC PDSX PFGH>
        when a04 = WTRB, then <a05-a07> = <PTRB PDSX PRGH>
        when a04 = WTRC, then <a05-a07> = <PTRC PDSX PFGH> }
```

The key difference between the two possibilities within the claim's possibility set is whether Amy willing the administration of treatment A to Pat results in Amy perceiving that treatment A was administered to Pat or Amy perceiving that treatment C was administered to Pat.

This book does not contain a trace where Amy's decision basis reflects a state of uncertainty as to the accurate realization of her will. This book also does not contain a trace where Amy's will is unrealized during the decision implementation phase.

Appendix B. Describing the Norm

In Trace 5.1 on page 32, Amy describes her decision basis norm to Zoë as:

```
a09:
  α ∈ {
    ADTR rox I/O ::
      when a04 = WTRA, then <a05-a07> = <PTRA PDSX PDED>
      when a04 = WTRB, then <a05-a07> = <???? ???? ????>
      when a04 = WTRC, then <a05-a07> = <???? ???? ????> }
```

This is an *incomplete* description of Amy's norm. A *complete* description would allow Zoë to enumerate the norm's reference set. This appendix provides an example of a reference set consistent with Amy's description of her norm. There are many other reference sets also consistent with Amy's norm description.

In this example, Amy believes that the state spaces associated with the variables in her consequence are:

```
a05 ∈ {PTRA PTRB PTRC}
a06 ∈ {PDSX PDSY}
a07 ∈ {PDED PCRI PMDI PFGH PRGH}
```

Amy's norm description can be rewritten as:

```
a09:
  α ∈ {
    ADTR rox I/O ::
      when a04 = WTRA, then <a05-a07> = <PTRA PDSX PDED>
      when a04 = WTRB, then <a05-a07> = <aaaa bbbb cccc>
      when a04 = WTRC, then <a05-a07> = <dddd eeee ffff> }
```

There are six variables in this template: aaaa to ffff.

Amy therefore believes that:

```
aaaa ∈ {PTRA PTRB PTRC}
bbbb ∈ {PDSX PDSY}
cccc ∈ {PDED PCRI PMDI PFGH PRGH}
dddd ∈ {PTRA PTRB PTRC}
eeee ∈ {PDSX PDSY}
ffff ∈ {PDED PCRI PMDI PFGH PRGH}
```

The norm's reference set is the cartesian product of the state spaces associated with each of these six variables. The cardinality of the reference set is $(3 \times 2 \times 5) \times (3 \times 2 \times 5) = 900$.

A method of enumerating the reference set is to iterate these variables in the order aaaa to ffff. The first few elements of the enumeration are:

```
ADTR rox I/O ::
  when a04 = WTRA, then <a05-a07> = <PTRA PDSX PDED>
  when a04 = WTRB, then <a05-a07> = <PTRA PDSX PDED>
  when a04 = WTRC, then <a05-a07> = <PTRA PDSX PDED>
ADTR rox I/O ::
  when a04 = WTRA, then <a05-a07> = <PTRA PDSX PDED>
  when a04 = WTRB, then <a05-a07> = <PTRB PDSX PDED>
  when a04 = WTRC, then <a05-a07> = <PTRA PDSX PDED>
ADTR rox I/O ::
  when a04 = WTRA, then <a05-a07> = <PTRA PDSX PDED>
  when a04 = WTRB, then <a05-a07> = <PTRC PDSX PDED>
  when a04 = WTRC, then <a05-a07> = <PTRA PDSX PDED>
ADTR rox I/O ::
  when a04 = WTRA, then <a05-a07> = <PTRA PDSX PDED>
  when a04 = WTRB, then <a05-a07> = <PTRA PDSY PDED>
  when a04 = WTRC, then <a05-a07> = <PTRA PDSX PDED>
ADTR rox I/O ::
  when a04 = WTRA, then <a05-a07> = <PTRA PDSX PDED>
  when a04 = WTRB, then <a05-a07> = <PTRB PDSY PDED>
  when a04 = WTRC, then <a05-a07> = <PTRA PDSX PDED>
```

The last few elements of the enumeration are:

```
ADTR rox I/O ::
  when a04 = WTRA, then <a05-a07> = <PTRA PDSX PDED>
  when a04 = WTRB, then <a05-a07> = <PTRB PDSX PRGH>
  when a04 = WTRC, then <a05-a07> = <PTRC PDSY PRGH>
ADTR rox I/O ::
  when a04 = WTRA, then <a05-a07> = <PTRA PDSX PDED>
  when a04 = WTRB, then <a05-a07> = <PTRC PDSX PRGH>
  when a04 = WTRC, then <a05-a07> = <PTRC PDSY PRGH>
ADTR rox I/O ::
  when a04 = WTRA, then <a05-a07> = <PTRA PDSX PDED>
  when a04 = WTRB, then <a05-a07> = <PTRA PDSY PRGH>
  when a04 = WTRC, then <a05-a07> = <PTRC PDSY PRGH>
ADTR rox I/O ::
  when a04 = WTRA, then <a05-a07> = <PTRA PDSX PDED>
  when a04 = WTRB, then <a05-a07> = <PTRB PDSY PRGH>
  when a04 = WTRC, then <a05-a07> = <PTRC PDSY PRGH>
ADTR rox I/O ::
  when a04 = WTRA, then <a05-a07> = <PTRA PDSX PDED>
  when a04 = WTRB, then <a05-a07> = <PTRC PDSY PRGH>
  when a04 = WTRC, then <a05-a07> = <PTRC PDSY PRGH>
```

All elements of the norm's reference set share the subclaim:

```
  when a04 = WTRA, then <a05-a07> = <PTRA PDSX PDED>
```

This will be true of any reference set consistent with Amy's description of her decision basis norm.

Appendix C. Predicting the Utility Function

The decision model employed in this book can support situations where the DM may mispredict its utility function. The need for this capability for some decision problems is indicated by the adage, "Success is getting what you want. Happiness is wanting what you get."

For example, two changes must be made to Trace 8.1 on page 61 to support utility function prediction. First, Amy's decision basis must be expanded to explicitly include the result of employing her *predicted* utility function:

```
-- t: 020 --
Amy:
  a01:
    α ∈ {
      ADTR rox I/O ::
        when a04 = WTRA, then <a05-a08> = <PTRA PDSX PDED U000>
        when a04 = WTRB, then <a05-a08> = <PTRB PDSX PRGH U004>
        when a04 = WTRC, then <a05-a08> = <PTRC PDSX PFGH U003>
      ADTR rox I/O ::
        when a04 = WTRA, then <a05-a08> = <PTRA PDSY PDED U000>
        when a04 = WTRB, then <a05-a08> = <PTRB PDSY PCRI U001>
        when a04 = WTRC, then <a05-a08> = <PTRC PDSY PDED U000> }
```

U000 means utility 0, U001 means utility 1, and so forth.

Second, the decision implementation phase must add a step where Amy's *actual* utility function is used to map her perception of Pat's post-treatment state into her actual utility:

```
==== DECISION IMPLEMENTATION PHASE ====

-- t: 040 --
Amy:
  a04: WTRB


-- t: 041 --

-- t: 042 --
Amy:
  a05: PTRB


-- t: 043 --

-- t: 044 --
Amy:
  a06: PDSX


-- t: 045 --

-- t: 046 --
Amy:
  a07: PRGH


-- t: 047 --
Amy:
  a08: U000
```

These two changes allow an inconsistency to arise between Amy's *predicted* utility function as employed in the construction of her decision basis and her *actual* utility function as experienced during decision implementation. In this example, Amy's decision basis predicted that she would experience high utility (4) after perceiving Pat's state as *robust good health*, but during decision implementation she experienced low utility instead (0). Amy would evaluate her decision basis as *false* for mispredicting her utility function.

Appendix D. List of Abbreviations

ADTR	Administer Treatment [Decision Problem]
AMDM	Autonomous Machine Decision Maker
DBET	Decision Basis Evaluation Testbed
DM	Decision Maker
DMA	Decision Making Algorithm
E	Eliminated [Alternative]
I/O	Input / Output
PRNG	Pseudo-Random Number Generator
PSS	[Alternative Set] Partition Subset
R	Retained [Alternative]
UMC	Utility Maximization Count
UMN	Utility Maximum - No
UMY	Utility Maximum - Yes

· Token shape abbreviations are listed in Chapter 2.

· ADTR-specific abbreviations are listed in Chapter 4.

Bibliography

[1] Bostrom, Nick. (2014). *Superintelligence: Paths, Dangers, Strategies.* Oxford: Oxford University Press.

[2] Collins, J., Hall, N., & Paul, L.A. (2004). *Causation and Counterfactuals.* Cambridge, MA: Bradford Books.

[3] Gärdenfors, Peter. (1988). Knowledge in Flux: Modeling the Dynamics of Epistemic States. Cambridge, MA: MIT Press.

[4] Klein, Gary. (1998). *Sources of Power: How People Make Decisions.* Cambridge, MA: MIT Press.

[5] Lawrence, David B. (1999). *The Economic Value of Information.* New York: Springer-Verlag.

[6] Peterson, Martin. (2009). *An Introduction to Decision Theory.* New York: Cambridge University Press.

Index

www.ingramcontent.com/pod-product-compliance
Lightning Source LLC
Chambersburg PA
CBHW080410060326
40689CB00019B/4194